AF594637

★ SECOND EDITION ★

Immortal Moments
IN CARDINALS HISTORY

FAMOUS AND FORGOTTEN HIGHLIGHTS OF THE ST. LOUIS CARDINALS

ROBERT L. TIEMANN
INTRODUCTION AND CONTRIBUTIONS BY RON JACOBER

Copyright © 2024, Reedy Press, LLC
All rights reserved.
Reedy Press
PO Box 5131
St. Louis, MO 63139
www.reedypress.com

No part of this publication may be reproduced or transmitted in any form or by any means, electronic or mechanical, including photocopy, recording, or any information storage and retrieval system, without permission in writing from the publisher. Permissions may be sought directly from Reedy Press at the above mailing address or via our website at www.reedypress.com.

Library of Congress Control Number: 2023938770

ISBN: 9781681064802

All front and back cover images are courtesy of Getty Images.
All interior images are believed to be in the public domain unless otherwise noted.

Printed in the United States of America
24 25 26 27 28 5 4 3 2 1

TABLE OF CONTENTS

Courtesy Missouri Historical Society, St. Louis

INTRODUCTION

Opening Day *n.*: the day on which the regular season opens.

That's the definition in the *Baseball Dictionary*. But if you're a member of what is lovingly called Cardinals Nation, opening day is a holy day of obligation. It's a day to celebrate the greatest game on earth in the best baseball town in the world. It's the end of another long, gray winter. Another renewal of life. All is well. Until a long losing streak!

The St. Louis Cardinals have played more than 22,500 games, every one unique in some way. There are so many great stories and so many terrific athletes who have donned the St. Louis uniform over the last 140 years. Scores of books have been written about the Redbirds but none like *Immortal Moments in Cardinals History*.

Even the most rabid Cardinals fan will discover fascinating stories they've never heard. For example, did you know there was a Cardinals team that helped rescue injured passengers from a train wreck? You may know that the team known as the Browns eventually became the Cardinals, but did you know they were also known as the Perfectos and that a later version of the Browns moved to Baltimore and became the Orioles?

Where were you on September 8, 1998? There were 43,698 of you at Busch Stadium (though 200,000 claim they were there!). In the fourth inning, Mark McGwire hit the first pitch he saw from the Chicago Cubs' Kent Mercker over the left field wall for home run number 62, breaking Roger Maris's celebrated single-season home run record. Mike Shannon made the call on the KMOX radio broadcast. Hall of Fame broadcaster Jack Buck, standing next to Mike, said a couple minutes later, "I'm happy you got to call it, Mike." A brief man-hug followed. Tears filled Jack's eyes. McGwire finished the record-shattering season with 70 home runs.

Then, there was the epic and improbable home run on October 14, 1985, off the bat of Ozzie Smith in game 5 of the National League Championship series against the Los Angeles Dodgers' Tom Niedenfuer. Smith had not hit a home run left-handed in 3,009 at bats until that one that will long be remembered as the "Go Crazy" home run because of Jack Buck's call on the broadcast.

You'll also learn about star players often forgotten. Many Redbird fans know about the exploits of Albert, Tatis, Yadi, Eckstein, and Edmonds, but few people are aware that a guy nicknamed "The Rajah" was the best right-handed hitter in Cardinals history and maybe the best in baseball history. He hit over .400 three times, including .424 once. The Rajah gets his due here.

Cardinals history isn't all about the stars. Take, for instance, the unlikely story of Larry Jaster. Larry shut out the Dodgers five times in one season but won only 35

Courtesy Don Korte

big-league games before his career ended at age 28. Or consider Bob Forsch, who threw two no-hitters—something Bob Gibson never did. Then again, Gibby, the greatest Cardinals pitcher in their long history, accomplished feats other pitchers could only dream about.

This book doesn't neglect the club's great managers. Since 1882, there have been 63, although that number can be misinterpreted. Some were successful but others were major-league failures. The 1890 team had five different managers. Arlie Latham was at the helm for three games in 1896—and lost all three! In 1958, Stan Hack managed just 10 games and lost seven of them. And in later years, Jack Krol managed two different times as interim manager for a total of three games. He was 1 and 2.

One of the more interesting characters to manage was Charles Comiskey, probably best known as the owner of the Chicago White Sox. He managed the Cardinals for eight different seasons. His teams won 563 games and lost 273, giving Comiskey a better winning percentage than Hall of Famers Red Schoendienst, Whitey Herzog, and Tony La Russa. But ask an old-timer, "Who's the best manager in history?" and the answer might be Billy Southworth. In the early 1940s, his teams won more than 100 games in three consecutive seasons and won two World Series.

I am lucky enough to have experienced memorable moments both as a fan and as a professional. As a young sportscaster at Channel 5 (KSD-TV in those days), I was sent to interview famous Cards announcer Harry Caray after he learned Anheuser-Busch would not renew his contract. I went to look for Harry with a TV crew and found him midafternoon at Busch's Grove in west St. Louis County. When I walked in, Harry said, "Ron, have a Schlitz!" I declined but asked if he would do an interview. He said, loudly, "Hell, yes!" So the cameraman came in and set up. Harry insisted on doing the interview holding the can of Schlitz next to his head. He proceeded to unload, and the interview aired on Channel 5 on the six o'clock news. Immediately after the newscast, an A-B official called and strongly "suggested" the interview not air again that night. But it did at 10 o'clock and again the next day several times. Years later, when I saw Harry in the Cubs broadcast booth, he said, "Ron, I made you famous!" I responded, "No, Harry, you made me infamous."

Courtesy Don Korte

I've never met a Cardinals fan, a true Cardinals fan, who doesn't remember the David Freeze home run in game 6 of the 2011 World Series against Texas. It sent thousands of Rangers fans into serious depression. Rumor has it that some of them moved to Mexico! Three times the Rangers were within one strike of winning the game and the World Series. I recall that a sports psychologist told me on the pregame broadcast before game 7 that there was no way Texas could win after the way they lost game 6 and the Freeze home run. How right he was. It's one of the great Cardinals moments that will remain immortal.

The name "David Freeze" is *frozen* in Cardinals lore. But, how about 99 years earlier? Dizzy Dean and his brother Paul pitching both ends of a doubleheader and nearly throwing two no-hitters against the Brooklyn Dodgers? Or the big-league promotion of Stan Musial, who hit a mere .426 in his first 12 games after being called up from the minors? He made several spectacular plays in right field, prompting the Chicago Cubs manager to say, "Nobody, but nobody, can be that good." Well, the kid from Donora, Pennsylvania, was that good. Did you know that Stan "The Man," as Brooklyn Dodgers fans called him, had 1,815 hits at home *and* 1,815 hits on the road? You can't make things like that up . . . but as Casey Stengel used to say, "You can look it up." Readers of this second editon of *Immortal Moments in Cardinals History* won't have to.

—Ron Jacober

Courtesy Missouri Historical Society, St. Louis

THIS is how the downtown streets appeared after a few minutes of the pandemonium that was spontaneous upon receipt of news that the Cardinals had clinched the pennant. Looking east along "Olive Street Canyon" where thousands of fragments of

Courtesy Missouri Historical Society, St. Louis

VON DER AHE BRINGS PRO BASEBALL BACK TO ST. LOUIS

May 2, 1882

The current Cardinals club has been in the National League since 1892, but it can trace its origins back ten more years to 1882, when the team was a member of the American Association, a separate major league. The team was called the Browns up until 1899 and didn't become known as the Cardinals until the 1900 season.

The first professional baseball club in St. Louis, the St. Louis Brown Stockings, was formed in 1875. The team led the National Association in attendance. The following year, the National League of Professional Base Ball Clubs replaced the National Association, and the Brown Stockings were one of the National League's founding members. The National League charged a minimum admission price of fifty cents, twice what the Brown Stockings had charged in 1875, and attendance plummeted locally. Following the 1877 season, the club disbanded.

For the next few years, independent teams held forth at the Grand Avenue grounds. An immigrant small businessman from Germany, Christian F. W. Von der Ahe, owned a grocery one block from the ballpark, and his hofbrau beer was sold there to thirsty patrons. After the games, players and spectators could repair to Von der Ahe's store to eat and drink in his beer garden. Although not versed in the fine points of baseball, Chris saw potential profit in the game and formed a corporation, the Sportsman's Park and Club. It took over the lease of the Grand Avenue ball field in 1881 and made Sportsman's Park a popular destination for baseball and other amusements.

In 1882, Von der Ahe was one of six independent operators who banded together to form the American Association as a rival to the National League. Unlike the NL, the association allowed 25 cent admissions, beer sales, and Sunday games, all of which squared nicely with Von der Ahe's business model. Chris and his corporation invested $2,000 in improvements to the park and budgeted $7,900 for players' salaries.

Courtesy Missouri Historical Society, St. Louis

The new pro team, called the Browns, was put together and run by Ned Cuthbert, an original Brown from 1875 who had stayed in town. He relied on several locals, but among the players he brought in was 22 year-old Charlie Comiskey. A first baseman, Comiskey would become the most famous Brown of them all as captain/manager/first baseman/cleanup hitter of a perennial championship club.

The 1882 season opened with a three-game series, May 2, 3, and 4, against the Eclipse Club of Louisville. The Browns swept the set, with two of the games being pitched by big George McGinnis from nearby Alton. Although the Browns finished fifth out of six teams in the standings, the club led the circuit in attendance. Big league baseball was back in St. Louis to stay.

Von der Ahe knew very little about baseball, but he knew beer and soon figured out that baseball sells beer. So he bought the Browns.

BROWNS WIN 27 STRAIGHT AT HOME

July 16, 1885

After finishing fifth, second, and fourth in the first three seasons of American Association play, the St. Louis Browns won their first pennant in 1885. Playing in an eight team league with a 112-game schedule, St. Louis finished with a 79–33 record and a whopping sixteen-game margin over second-place Cincinnati. The feature of the year was a streak of 27 consecutive victories at home, a major league record that still stands more than a century and a quarter later.

Meddlesome owner Chris Von der Ahe had seen three different managers quit in those first three seasons, so for 1885 he assumed the title of manager himself. Captain Charles Comiskey was left in charge of the team on the field, and his early success kept Von der Ahe from demanding unnecessary changes. Comiskey relied on two young pitchers who had each debuted in the last half of 1884, Dave Foutz and Bob Caruthers. The Browns opened the season at home and split the first six games before winning the finale of the homestand on April 26. After a short road swing, the team returned to Sportsman's Park and went 14–0 in home games versus the association's eastern clubs.

After a five-week, seven-city road trip, the first-place Browns started six weeks of home games on July 3. In the morning game of a split doubleheader on the Fourth of July, the Browns needed extra innings to beat the last-place Orioles 7–2, Caruthers pitching his 20th win of the season. In the nightcap, Foutz had a 2–0 lead going into the bottom of the ninth before being touched for a single and a triple. But he got the next three outs for a 2–1 win, his 17th.

A road trip? How about five weeks and seven cities in the middle of a 27-game home winning streak.

The winning streak continued through the Baltimore and Brooklyn series and reached 12 in a row with three wins versus the Athletics. The final game of the string came on July 16. Comiskey gave little-used veteran Jim McGinnis just his sixth pitching assignment of the season, and his teammates gave him a 9–1 lead after an inning and a half. But the Athletics fought back behind the incredible hitting of Harry Stovey, who had three doubles before hitting a game-tying home run in the seventh inning. Substitutions were illegal back then, but players already in the game could switch positions, and Comiskey then brought Foutz in from left field to pitch. It would be the only game all season in which the Browns used two pitchers. Foutz hurled two scoreless innings and the Browns won the game 13–1 with two runs in the top of the ninth. St. Louis's record stood at 47–17, good for a nine and a half game lead. Foutz would lose the next day, 8–3, to snap the winning streak at 12 games overall and 27 games at home.

Courtesy Missouri Historical Society, St. Louis

All images courtesy Library of Congress

THE WORLD'S CHAMPIONS
ONE PACKED IN EACH BOX OF
TEN CIGARETTES

BASE BALL PLAYERS.
CHAS. W. BENNETT.
JOHN M. WARD.
MIKE KELLY.

OARSMEN.

PUGILISTS.
JOHN L. SULLIVAN.
JAKE KILRAIN.
JEM SMITH.
CHARLIE MITCHELL.
JIMMY CARNEY.
JACK DEMPSEY.
IKE WEIR.

WELCH - C. FIELD - ST. LOUIS.

ST LOUIS
Welsh
BROWN'S

WELCH'S RUN WRAPS UP WORLD SERIES TRIUMPH

October 23, 1886

In 1885, the Chicago White Stockings, champions of the National League, had agreed to play the American Association champion St. Louis Browns in a postseason series to determine the best team in the land. The series was to travel to several cities, but it ended in a rancorous feud between the two teams after just seven of the planned 12 games were played. The Browns claimed victory, but the White Stockings insisted that the series finished even, three games to three with one tie.

When the same two clubs repeated as pennant winners in 1886, another series was arranged. As negotiated by St. Louis owner Chris Von der Ahe and Chicago owner Albert Spalding, this series would be restricted to a best-of-seven competition with games in the two home cities. A seventh game, if necessary, would be played at a neutral site. With both teams eager to prove themselves, the owners agreed to give the winning club the entire gate receipts (minus umpiring expenses) while leaving the losers with nothing but wounded pride.

The first three games were played in Chicago with the home team taking two out of three. The Browns won the next two games, played in St. Louis, to set up a potential series-clinching game on Saturday, October 23.

Despite ominous clouds and a light rain, close to 8,000 St. Louis fans came out hoping to celebrate. Injuries had left the Chicago pitching staff decimated, so Captain Adrian Anson had little choice but to start his ace, John Clarkson, for the fourth time in the week. He was opposed by St. Louis star Bob Caruthers, making his third start in five days. Caruthers was touched for single runs in the second, fourth, and sixth innings, with Chicago second baseman Fred Pfeffer scoring each time.

Courtesy Library of Congress

Clarkson held St. Louis to one hit and no runs through seven innings. But the Browns broke through with a sudden three-run rally in the bottom of the eighth to tie the game. Arlie Latham delivered the big blow, a game-tying, two-out, two-run triple that was misplayed by left fielder Abner Dalrymple.

With the score still 3–3 in the bottom of the tenth, Curt Welch led off with a clean single to center. A fumble by the shortstop put another man on, and a sacrifice bunt left Welch, the winning run, just 90 feet from home. With light-hitting Doc Bushong at bat, Clarkson unfurled a high wild pitch, which catcher King Kelly could barely touch. The ball went to the backstop, and Welch trotted home with the run that made the Browns undisputed world champions. The club reaped the total gate of $13,781.95, and owner Von der Ahe gave half of it to the players, who each got about $580 for their share.

> ***This gave the American Association its only clear-cut World Series victory over the National League.***

TIP O'NEILL HITS FOR THE CYCLE ON CONSECUTIVE SATURDAYS

April 30, 1887; May 7, 1887

In the heyday of the powerhouse St. Louis Browns teams of the 1880s, the premier hitter on the squad was Tip O'Neill, the right fielder and number three batter in the batting order. Since then, St. Louis lineups have sported some impressive number-three hitters (Hornsby, Sisler, Musial, and Pujols, to name a few). But none of those latter-day superstars was able to reach the batting marks that Tip O'Neill put in place in 1887, his greatest season. The year 1887 was the only year in which the batter was given four strikes on a strikeout (it took five balls to walk), and it was the only year in which bases on balls were counted officially as hits. Playing in the American Association, O'Neill led the circuit in hits, runs, RBIs, and batting average. He also led the league in doubles, triples, and home runs, making him the only man in big league history to lead his league in all three categories of extra-base hits. His 1887 batting average has been listed as high as .492 and as low as .435, depending on whether you count walks as hits or not. Over the course of the season he had two six-for-seven games (with one base on balls in each), plus five five-hit games and more than a dozen four-hit performances.

Born and raised in Upper Canada (now Ontario), O'Neill broke into pro baseball as a pitcher. After he joined the Browns at age twenty-five in 1884, Captain Comiskey was quick to shift him to left field to maximize his hitting ability. While the prevailing style of bat in those days was a long, heavy "wagon tongue," O'Neill wielded a tiny stick, barely over thirty inches long. But, boy, could he connect with it!

In a 28–11 St. Louis victory over visiting Cleveland on April 30, Tip bashed two home runs and still was able to hit for an 1887-style cycle, adding a walk, a single, a double, and a triple to finish the day six for seven. The 28 run total still stands as a St. Louis record (tied once by the Cardinals in 1929). The Browns totaled 36 hits, although 10 were actually bases on balls. Teammate Billy Gleason was officially seven for seven in that game, although four of his "hits" were walks.

The rules also gave the home team the choice of which team batted first, and the Browns opted to take the first crack. O'Neill was retired in his first trip to the plate. In the third inning, he walked and scored. It wasn't until the fourth inning, when the Browns plated five runs, that Tip finally got his first clean hit, a single to center. Batting twice in the nine-run fifth, O'Neill homered "down behind the bulletin

Courtesy Library of Congress

board" in center field, then tripled with "a beautiful drive" to left. During the eight-run sixth, Tip poled another home run "under the seats at the left field fence." In his final at-bat in the eighth inning, he produced a double. Since the Browns were batting first, he might have gotten another chance in the ninth inning, but the umpire called the game after eight innings due to darkness. Since substitutions were not allowed, Mike Morrison pitched the complete game for the losers.

Exactly one week later, on May 7, O'Neill "cycled" again, going five for five with a walk, single, double, triple, and homer against Guy Hecker of the Louisville Colonels to pace a 12–7 St. Louis win. Tip drove in the first run of the game in the top of the first with a triple into the left field seats and scored on a fly ball. (The rules allowed fielders to go into the stands after balls in those days). After a walk in the third, O'Neill got an infield hit to shortstop in the fifth and scored again. The score was tied when he batted with a man on in the seventh, and this time he lifted a drive "over the left field fence" (i.e., over the back fence and out of the park) for a two-run homer. And in the eighth he doubled to left and scored another run.

Courtesy Library of Congress

Courtesy Library of Congress

COPYRIGHTED 1888 BY GOODWIN & CO. NY

J. E. O'NEIL; L.F.-St Louis Browns.

OLD JUDGE CIGARETTES Goodwin & Co., New York.

Tip was called Canada's Babe Ruth. He is in the Canadian Baseball Hall of Fame but not in the Hall at Cooperstown.

Jos. Hall, Photo, 111 Fulton St., Brooklyn, N.Y.

St. Louis Ball Club, 1888.

World Champions 1885, 1886, 1887

. Boyle. 4. Lyon. 7. Comisky. 10. Knouff.
. O'Neil. 5. McGarr. 8. McCarty. 11. Latham
12. Hudson
13. Robinso

King P. St. Louis Browns

LD JUDGE CIGARETTES Goodwin & Co., New York.

McCarthy C.F. St. Louis Brown's

OLD JUDGE CIGARETTES Goodwin & Co., New York.

Robinson. S.S. St. Louis Browns

UDGE CIGARETTES Goodwin & New Yor

Courtesy Library of Congress

SWEEP ASSURES BROWNS OF FOURTH STRAIGHT PENNANT

September 30, 1888

After the St. Louis Browns were trounced in the 1887 World Series, owner Chris Von der Ahe decided to peddle some of his biggest stars. Former 40-game winners Dave Foutz and Bob Caruthers were sold to the Brooklyn Bridegrooms, along with catcher Doc Bushong. Shortstop Bill Gleason and center fielder Curt Welch went to the Athletics.

It was up to Captain Charlie Comiskey to fill the holes, and few observers gave the Browns much of a chance to repeat as four-time pennant winners in 1888. Somehow, Commy pulled it off. Young Charles "Silver" King, a St. Louis native in just his second year with the team, carried the pitching staff, often pitching with just one day of rest. Right fielder Tommy McCarthy, a 23-year-old National League washout, fit perfectly in the Browns' renowned aggressive racehorse style. The team overtook first-place Brooklyn in June. The lead seesawed in July, but the Browns pulled away in August. The triumphant moment of the championship season came in the last three days of September, when St. Louis swept three games from visiting Brooklyn.

The series opened on Friday, and Silver King was at his best, hitting one batter but walking no one in a two-hit, 7–0 shutout. Comiskey, Arlie Latham, and Nate Hudson each drove home two runs, as the Browns snapped Brooklyn rookie Mickey Hughes's six-game winning streak. In the Saturday game, Comiskey shellacked Foutz's serves for five hits himself. Elton Chamberlain, a late-season acquisition to the pitching staff, held Brooklyn to six hits and won easily, 7–4.

The Sunday finale brought 13,269 paying customers out to Sportsman's Park, easily the largest crowd of the season, with an overflow standing in the outfield in front of the bleachers. The Browns chose to bat first and were retired when Tip O'Neill's foul tip out was turned into a quick double play. The Bridegrooms got four hits in the bottom of the first off King, but McCarthy threw two different runners out at home to limit the damage to just one run. In the fourth, Brooklyn hurler Hughes became flustered by the umpiring and issued four bases on balls. O'Neill, McCarthy, and Jack Boyle chipped in with hits, giving St. Louis three runs and the lead. The Browns added pairs of runs in each of the next two innings, and then piled up four in the eighth and two in the ninth to win by a final score of 13–4. Hughes gave a total of 12 bases on balls, four of them to pesky Yank Robinson, the second-place hitter in the home team lineup. Batting third, O'Neill had four of the Browns' 14 hits, and cleanup man Comiskey drove home three mates. King picked up his 44th win of the season, walking only one while allowing nine hits.

Courtesy Library of Congress

The Grooms left town 10½ games behind with just 11 to play. The Browns mathematically clinched the pennant two days later.

Home field advantage? The Browns played 81 games at home and only 54 on the road. They were 60 and 21 at home.

BREITENSTEIN HURLS NO-HITTER IN FIRST START

October 4, 1891

In the St. Louis franchise's first years in the National League in the 1890s, the team's best player was pitching mainstay Ted Breitenstein. The left-hander is credited with leading the league in games and innings pitched, complete games, losses, walks, and earned run average in various seasons during his five full years with the Browns, 1892–1896. A native of St. Louis, he actually first made headlines on the final day of the 1891 American Association season when he pitched a no-hitter for the Browns against the Louisville Colonels in his very first major league starting assignment.

The freckle-faced redhead had gained a measure of local acclaim in 1889, when he pitched a local amateur team, the Home Comforts, to the city championship, but he did not sign a professional contract with the Browns until 1891. Captain Charlie Comiskey gave him a brief look early in the season and then farmed him out to Grand Rapids in the Northwestern League.

Recalled at the end of the minor league season, he pitched in relief in five games for Comiskey before getting a chance to start at Sportsman's Park in the first game of a Sunday doubleheader on October 4, 1891. It was the final date of the regular season for the second-place Browns, and a cold wind cut through the grounds. The opponents were the seventh-place Colonels, and a decent crowd, reported variously from 2,000–5,000 fans, came out for the season finale. Home team captain Comiskey chose for the team to bat first, as usual, and Dummy Hoy led off by being hit by a pitch. Tommy McCarthy followed with a one-out single, and Tip O'Neill's double drove home both runners to give Breitenstein an early 2–0 lead.

The southpaw retired the first two Louisville hitters before walking the third batter, Harry Taylor, who was quickly caught stealing by catcher John Munyan. That would be the only man to reach base against the youngster. Starting with cleanup hitter and future Hall of Famer Hugh Jennings in the second inning, Breitenstein retired the last 24 batters he faced. Although he later developed an overhand drop curve, an inshoot, and a change of pace, Breitenstein was a fastball pitcher first and foremost. In this first start, he struck out five hitters, including former Double A batting champion William Wolf (nicknamed "Jimmy" or "Chicken" Wolf) twice. The Browns played errorless defense behind him, and no especially difficult plays were mentioned in the newspaper accounts of the game. Louisville rookie Jouett Meekin, on the other hand, had all sorts of difficulties, walking six while throwing three wild pitches. And the Louisville catchers had four passed balls, making for an easy 8–0 St. Louis victory.

St. Louis's own Ted Breitenstein was on his way to stardom.

Called up from the minors, the St. Louis native started the first game of a final day doubleheader and threw a no-no against Louisville. He won 27 games the next season.

BROWNS BRING SUNDAY BASEBALL TO THE NATIONAL LEAGUE

April 17, 1892

The American Association was founded before the 1882 season to offer an alternative to the older and more sanctimonious National League. The association offered a cheaper minimum admission (25 cents as opposed to 50 cents) and allowed clubs to sell liquor at its parks and to play games on Sundays if legal in their cities. After a decade of uneasy coexistence, the NL and the AA engaged in a contract war in 1891 and into the winter of 1892. The St. Louis Browns were particularly hard hit by raids on their roster, and most of the team's stars jumped to NL clubs. Finally ready to concede defeat, the AA agreed to merge four of its teams into an expanded NL.

But Browns owner Chris Von der Ahe got several major concessions in the deal, including the right to play Sunday ball. Blue laws in most of the East Coast states made paid amusements illegal on the Sabbath, and eastern NL clubs were given the option of refusing to play Sunday road games. But in the more liberal Midwest, cities with large German populations like Cincinnati, St. Louis, Chicago, and Louisville were prime targets for Sunday ball. Appropriately, the first Sunday game played in the National League, which had been around since 1876, was played by the Browns in St. Louis on Easter Sunday, April 17, 1892, against the Cincinnati Reds.

The Browns had opened at home the previous Tuesday against the Chicago Colts (later to be known as the Cubs), drawing a crowd of 8,160. The Reds game the following Sunday drew at least 5,000 more than that (figures of 13,300 and 15,200 were published in the papers), much to the delight of Von der Ahe and Cincinnati owner John Brush. Over the course of the season, their two clubs would lead the league in attendance, thanks almost entirely to their Sunday gates.

That pioneering Sunday game put the St. Louis fans into something of a quandary. The home team consisted almost entirely of players brought in from other clubs. Only pitcher Bob Caruthers had any local history, having starred for the Browns in the mid-1880s before spending four years with the Brooklyn Bridegrooms. The visiting Reds, however, had a lineup heavy with old St. Louis favorites. Captain Charlie Comiskey and left fielder Tip O'Neill had been mainstays with the Browns in 1891 and for years before. Third baseman Arlie Latham had played for St. Louis from 1883 to 1889 and was still wildly popular for his loudmouthed wit and his animated coaching antics. Reds pitcher Tony Mullane had nearly pitched the Browns to a pennant back in 1883. Both squads came in for much applause that day, with the Reds winning 5–1 thanks to three home runs, quite a rare power display for the era.

Courtesy Missouri Historical Society, St. Louis

Never on Sunday? So-called "blue laws" prevented any athletic games on the Sabbath. But Von der Ahe ignored them and the Browns played on Easter Sunday. East Coast teams had the option of refusing to play on Sundays.

CY YOUNG AND THE PERFECTOS COME TO TOWN

April 15, 1899

After a decade of success in the old American Association from 1882 to 1891, the St. Louis franchise's first seven seasons in the National League, 1892 to 1898, were a string of disappointments and disasters. Owner Chris Von der Ahe's Browns never finished higher than ninth in the 12-team National League. When a fire destroyed the Sportsman's Park grandstand in early 1898, Von der Ahe did not have enough insurance and eventually went bankrupt. The franchise was sold at sheriff's auction in March 1899 and quickly passed into the hands of two brothers who also owned the NL's Cleveland Spiders, Frank de Haas Robison and M. S. "Stanley" Robison.

The Spiders had had some on-the-field success, finishing in second place three times, but did very poorly at the box office, finishing last in home attendance in 1897 and 1898. Now that they owned two teams, the Robisons moved all their best players to St. Louis, leaving Cleveland with the dregs. The news was greeted with enthusiasm on the banks of the Mississippi, where fans were tired of the perennial ineptitude of Von der Ahe's Browns. The new team would abandon the time-honored brown stockings, adopting a cardinal red hue. In that first season of 1899, newspapers around the country dubbed the team the "Perfectos." The old name of Sportsman's Park

Courtesy Missouri Historical Society, St. Louis

Young played just 2 of his 22 years with St. Louis but pitched 72 complete games and posted 45 wins. He threw a stunning 690 innings in the two seasons.

Courtesy Library of Congress

was also dropped, with the improved ballpark rechristened League Park.

The nickname "Cardinals" would become the consensus choice of the local press the following winter, although its identification as a bird would not get official sanction until the early 1920s. League Park would later bear the names Robison Field (1912–1916) and Cardinal Field (1917–1920).

Despite damp, dismal weather, opening day in 1899 brought out an enthusiastic crowd that approached 15,000, the largest in St. Louis in several years. The Robisons had moved several famous players from Cleveland, including three Hall of Famers: leadoff man and batting champ Jesse Burkett, pitcher-turned-infielder Bobby Wallace, and incomparable pitcher Cy Young. Two other Perfectos were St. Louis-born, first baseman–manager Patsy Tebeau and catcher Jack O'Connor.

Eight of the nine men in the Cleveland lineup had played with St. Louis the previous summer, including pitcher Willie Sudhoff, another product of the St. Louis sandlots.

As expected, the new St. Louis nine won easily, 10–1. Cy Young pitched around four errors, and his teammates put together two big innings with the help of five errors by the Spiders. Old Cy pitched his usual, unflappable game and doubled to drive home the game's first run himself. He added an RBI single later and pitched a six-hitter.

Although the Perfectos finished a disappointing fifth out of twelve teams in 1899, they had given renewed hope to a despondent baseball city. The Cleveland Spiders, meanwhile, had the worst team in history, winning only 20 games and losing 134.

Mathewson was called the "Christian Gentleman" because he refused to pitch on Sundays. In his 24 straight wins against the Cardinals, the Giants outscored St. Louis 122–50.

Courtesy Library of Congress

CARDS SNAP 24-GAME LOSING STREAK VS. MATHEWSON

May 24, 1909

Roger Bresnahan had been a popular star catcher for the New York Giants from 1902 to 1908 and was thought to have fine managerial potential. After the St. Louis Cardinals finished in last place for the second consecutive season in 1908, they acquired the veteran catcher in a trade and installed him as player–manager before the 1909 season. Although the price was steep (included were the Cards' top pitcher, Bugs Raymond, and top power hitter, Red Murray), the St. Louis team had nowhere to go but up.

One of the earliest achievements of the new Cardinals regime came on the occasion of Bresnahan's first visit to New York as St. Louis manager, when the Cards finally snapped a record losing streak versus Giant ace pitcher Christy Mathewson.

The arrival of Bresnahan with his new team provided an occasion for celebration at the Polo Grounds. Before the opening game of the series on May 24, some of New York's most famous personages took turns honoring their former idol. He was given a huge floral display and a silver loving cup inscribed with the names of politicians (including New York mayor George B. McClellan Jr.), entertainers (including legendary actor George M. Cohan), and baseball people (New York owner John T. Brush and Giant manager John J. McGraw among them).

The Giants opened the series with Mathewson pitching. Dating back to June 15, 1904, the famous Big Six had won 24 games in a row versus St. Louis, establishing a record for consecutive wins against one opponent that still stands today. He had also saved another game in the streak. His wins included four extra-inning complete games and five shutouts.

Courtesy Library of Congress

In this 1909 game, the Cards lost an apparent run in the first inning when Al Shaw missed the plate sliding home on a double steal. Against Cardinal left-hander Johnny Lush, New York scored a run in the fourth inning on a walk, an error by the second baseman, and a weak throw home on a sacrifice fly. But Lush pitched out of trouble in the other early innings, as the Giants stranded 10 runners in the first five frames. St. Louis tied the game in the sixth when Ed Konetchy reached base on an error and came around on singles by Steve Evans and Chappie Charles. The two winning runs came in the seventh and were also unearned, when Giant second sacker Larry Doyle let a dribbler trickle past him as two men scored. Bresnahan himself gave New York an extra chance in the eighth inning when he dropped a foul pop, but Lush was equal to all emergencies and finished strong with a 3–1 win. Although Mathewson had allowed only six hits and no earned runs, Bresnahan's Cardinals had finally beaten him.

Courtesy Library of Congress

Courtesy Library of Congress

ST. LOUIS PLAYERS RESCUE TRAIN WRECK VICTIMS

July 11, 1911

Roger Bresnahan's St. Louis Cardinals were riding high, figuratively, when they boarded a train in Philadelphia on Monday, July 10, 1911. They had just won three out of four from the Phillies to knock the Quakers out of first place. And fifth-place St. Louis trailed first-place Chicago by only three games. With four games scheduled against the last-place Boston Rustlers, the Cardinals seemed poised to move up in the standings. By the time the sun rose the next morning, however, a train wreck had replaced thoughts of pennants and ball games with gruesome visions of death and suffering.

The team and its traveling party occupied two Pullman sleeper cars that were added to the Federal Express. This famous train ran from Washington, DC, to Boston and bypassed Manhattan. The cars were ferried around the island from Jersey City to the Bronx, then returned to the rails. From Philadelphia to Jersey City, the Cardinals' cars were near the head of the train. The ride was hot, noisy, and uncomfortable, prompting manager Bresnahan to request a move to the back of the train. This was accomplished at the Bronx docks.

With the train running late, the motorman raced to make up time in the wee hours of the morning. Just after 3:30 a.m., near Bridgeport, Connecticut, the train was going 60 miles per hour in a 15-mile-per-hour zone. The engine careened off the track and down an 18-foot embankment, pulling the front cars of the nine-car train down with it. The baggage cars and day coach were torn to pieces against the stone side of the embankment, and several Pullman cars behind were also smashed. Twelve people died and four dozen more were seriously hurt.

The Cardinals' cars stayed on the track, though the occupants were given a severe jolt. Dressed mostly in pajamas, the players hastily put on shoes and clamored out to survey the scene. Hearing the terrified screams and moans of those passengers trapped in the forward cars, they quickly swung into action. With Bresnahan barking out orders, the team began tearing away debris to free people from the tangled wreckage using axes, pry bars, and bare hands. For half an hour, the St. Louis contingent provided most of the muscle in the rescue effort until local help arrived. Bodies of the dead and injured were carried out and laid on the neighborhood lawns. Rube Geyer and Mike Mowrey were among the first to plunge into the work and were cited for special praise. But all agreed that Roger Bresnahan himself was the biggest hero. He was still wearing his pink pajamas, now black with soot and grime, when the team finally arrived in Boston on a special train later that day. The scheduled game was postponed, and the shaken and exhausted players retreated to their hotel.

Heroic rescue in pajamas! The Cardinals' Pullman cars were the only ones that stayed on the track. Manager Roger Bresnahan led the rescue that was credited with saving several lives.

Courtesy Library of Congress

CARDINALS FANS GET PENNANT FEVER

August 27, 1914

After decades of futility, the St. Louis Cardinals briefly flirted with first place in August 1914, and the local fans responded with two of the biggest crowds in franchise history up to that point. Cellar dwellers in 1913, the upstart Cardinals spurted toward the top in August.

When the New York team came to St. Louis on August 24, the Giants and Boston Braves were tied for first place with identical 59–48 records. The Cardinals had three more wins than either one (62) but five more losses (53). The first two Giant games were rained out, limiting the series to a doubleheader on Wednesday, August 26, and enthusiastic Cardinals fans flooded Robison Field. A crowd of more than 26,000 saw offsetting shutouts—Bill Doak won the opener 1–0 for St. Louis, and Christy Mathewson won 4–0 for New York in the second game.

Boston was next on the Robison Field schedule, and the home team won a 10-inning thriller, 3–2, on Thursday. The game was played on a dark, rainy day, and the Cards' first two runs came on inside-the-park home runs by Owen Wilson and Lee Magee. The winning run scored when the Braves left fielder lost a fly ball in the darkening mist, giving Cozy Dolan a walk-off double. The win put the Cardinals in second place, one game behind the Giants and a half game ahead of the Braves. It was the highest spot in the National League standings yet for a St. Louis club in August or later. Rain on Friday necessitated another doubleheader on Saturday.

Despite continued unseasonal weather, a new regular-season franchise record of 28,000 paid to see the twin bill. In the opener, the Braves pushed over their first two runs with successful squeeze bunts and won 4–0 behind a four-hitter by Bill James. In the nightcap, Cardinals ace Bill Doak had a 4–2 lead before walking the leadoff hitter in the eighth. In a controversial move, manager Miller Huggins yanked Doak in favor of Slim Sallee, his best left-hander. Slim struck out the first man but then walked two in a row, loading the bases. A long fly out brought home one Boston run, and then Rabbit Maranville hit one deep to center. In the darkness, outfielder Joe Riggert got a late break on the ball and it sailed over his head for a triple, giving the Braves a 5–4 lead. A wild pickoff throw made it 6–4, and the Cardinals went out in order in the bottom of the eighth before the umpires called the game because of darkness.

The Cards managed just one hit in losing the series finale on Sunday, and the St. Louis pennant bubble was burst. The team's third-place finish in 1914 was, however, its best since joining the National League in 1892.

Robison Field opened in 1893 (470 feet to left field, 500 feet to center). By 1909 the capacity was 21,000. When 28,000 showed up for a Sunday doubleheader, thousands stood in the playing field.

Courtesy Missouri Historical Society, St. Louis

Courtesy Don Korte

GONZALEZ STEALS HOME IN 15TH INNING

June 11, 1917

Mike Gonzalez is best remembered as the Cardinals third base coach whose stop sign was ignored by Enos Slaughter in the final game of the 1946 World Series. Never completely fluent in English, he also coined the famously succinct phrase "good field, no hit" to describe prospective players. That appellation might be applied to his own playing career, which ended with a .254 batting average and just 13 home runs in more than 1,000 games. His 52 career stolen bases are an indication that he could run fairly well—for a catcher.

But Miguel Angel Gonzalez Cordero, known as Mike Gonzalez in the US, was also one of the earliest Cubans to have a long career in the major leagues. His 16 seasons in the National League included three different stints as a Cardinals catcher: 1915–1918, 1924–1925, and 1931–1932. After retiring as a player, he coached for every St. Louis manager from 1934 to 1946.

Back in 1917, Gonzalez was in a batting slump well into the season and was seeing little playing time. On June 11, however, injuries forced manager Miller Huggins to juggle his lineup and insert Gonzalez at first base, batting second in the order.

Bill Doak was the Cardinals pitcher against the Phillies. In the top of the first inning, he gave up four runs on two hits and two bases on balls. The rally was abetted by an error on a wind-blown fly ball and a questionable check-swing ruling by the umpire. After that, Doak was brilliant, pitching 14 scoreless innings while allowing only four more hits and one more walk. The Cardinals tied the game with one run in the fourth inning and three in the sixth against Philadelphia hurler Joe Oeschger. Gonzalez had a chance to be a hero in the bottom of the ninth when he batted with two out and Jack Smith on second base. But he ignominiously struck out.

When Gonzalez batted in the 15th inning with no one on and one out, he was zero for six in the game, and his current slump had reached 2 for 38. But this time he got a solid hit to right, stretching it into a double when right fielder Gavvy Cravath let the ball get past him. He moved to third on a ground out, and Rogers Hornsby was intentionally walked, setting up a potential double steal. Hornsby lit out for second, but Phillie catcher Bill Killifer held the ball, forcing Gonzalez to stay at third. Undaunted, Gonzalez broke for home on Oeschger's next windup. Killifer took the high pitch and swiped a tag down as the runner was sliding across the plate. The ball came loose, and Gonzalez was safe with a steal of home to win the game, 5–4, just like Glenn Brummer two generations later.

Gonzalez resigned as a Cardinals coach in protest when some of the players who jumped to the Mexican League played in the Cuban winter league in 1946 with Gonzalez. Commissioner Happy Chandler ruled that any team that employed those who jumped would be banned from the majors. Gonzalez never returned to the US.

Courtesy Library of Congress

Courtesy Missouri Historical Society, St. Louis

Browns owner Phil Ball predicted there would be a World Series in Sportsman's Park by 1926, so he increased the capacity to 30,000. But it was the Cardinals not the Browns in the series in '26. They beat the Yankees in seven games. Babe Ruth was thrown out trying to steal second to end the series.

CARDINALS MOVE TO SPORTSMAN'S PARK

July 1, 1920

By 1916, the St. Louis Cardinals were the last remaining major league team with a wooden ballpark. They played at Vandeventer and Natural Bridge avenues on a plot that is now occupied by Beaumont High School. Chris Von der Ahe had moved his team there from Grand Avenue in 1893, and he brought the name "Sportsman's Park" with him. After a disastrous fire in 1898, Von der Ahe went bankrupt and the team passed into the hands of the Robison brothers, who rebuilt the park and renamed it "League Park." When the club and the grounds passed into the hands of Helene Robison Britton, daughter of one of the brothers, she rechristened it "Robison Field" in honor of her father and uncle. After she sold out to a group headed by James C. Jones, the Robison name was replaced by "Cardinal Field." But the old wooden grandstand, built after another fire in 1901, remained the same, and the club had no money to build a modern stadium.

When the American League moved a rival club into town in 1902, they took over the site of the original Sportsman's Park at Grand and Dodier avenues, and they also adopted the old nickname of "Browns." In 1909, the Browns revamped their Sportsman's Park, building a double-decked concrete and steel grandstand with adjoining concrete pavilion and bleachers. Finally, on June 24, 1920, they agreed to share Sportsman's Park with the Cardinals.

The first National League game at the newer Grand Avenue grounds took place on a sweltering Thursday, July 1. It was the annual Tuberculosis Society benefit, and a big crowd of 20,000 spectators was treated to a raft of pregame festivities. There were military bands from Jefferson Barracks and the Great Lakes Naval Training Station, a cabaret show, and a five-inning Army vs. Navy ball game. Lastly, the mayor handed out trophies to the winners of a junior marathon that finished with a lap around the ballpark.

In the regular game that followed, the visiting Pirates built a 2–0 lead against Cardinals lefty Ferdie Schupp before the Cards rallied late. Cliff Heathcote hit a home run into the right field bleachers in the eighth inning, and Austin McHenry's pinch single in the ninth sent the game to extra innings. But a throwing error by first baseman Jack Fournier opened the gates to a four-run Pirate 10th against reliever Willie Sherdel, and the Cardinals lost 6-2.

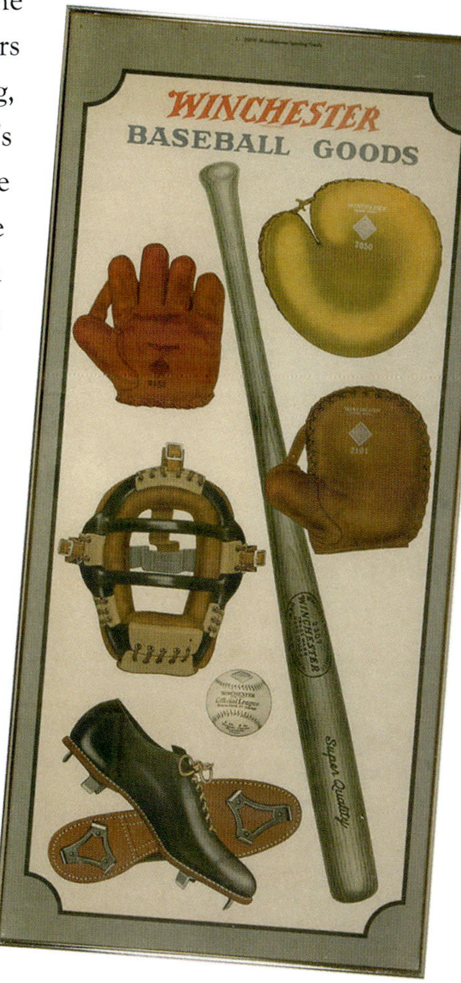

The move allowed the Cardinals to sell their plot on Natural Bridge and invest the money in minor league stock, spawning what would become Branch Rickey's famous farm system. The move also made a very happy man out of the St. Louis fire chief, who confessed to losing sleep on Saturday nights dreading the prospect of a fire at wooden Cardinal Field with a big Sunday crowd in attendance.

BOTH ST. LOUIS TEAMS LEAD BIG LEAGUES FOR FIRST TIME IN HISTORY

July 22, 1922

Courtesy Reedy Press

The *St. Louis Globe-Democrat* ran the headline on its front page on July 23, 1922. St. Louis baseball fans, downtrodden by three decades of bad ball clubs, were in ecstasy. Neither the Cardinals in the National League nor the Browns in the American League had ever won their league pennant. From 1892 to 1920, St. Louis had had 12 cellar dwellers and only six first-division teams. But the gloom had begun to lift. In 1921, both teams finished in third place. And finally in 1922, the sun burst through on two pennant contenders. The Browns passed the Yankees for first place in the AL race on June 16. On that date, the Cardinals were in second place, six and a half games behind the Giants.

Over the next five weeks, the Browns maintained a slim lead over New York, while the Cardinals went on a 27–9 tear that finally, on July 22, lifted them past the Giants and into first place as well. The Cards were paced by a potent batting attack in which all eight regulars finished the season hitting at least .292. The main man, of course, was second baseman Rogers Hornsby, who hit 42 home runs among his 250 hits, establishing new league records in each category.

Adding to the excitement was the fact that the Cardinals won each of the last five games of the first-place spurt in their final at-bats. On July 18, they tallied three in the eighth to grab a 9–7 lead over the Giants and held New York to one run in the top of the ninth for the win. That gave St. Louis the series, three games to one. On the next afternoon, Hornsby turned a seemingly certain defeat into a victory with a dramatic two-out, three-run home run in the bottom of the ninth, beating the Braves 9–8. On July 20, Boston and St. Louis battled into extra innings before the Cardinals won 5–4 on a tenth-inning, walk-off single by Del Gainer. On Friday, July 21, the game was scoreless through seven innings, and then the Braves got a run in the top of the eighth. The Cardinals came right back with six runs in their half to salt away the game. The best rally of all came on July 22. St. Louis was behind 8–3 going into the last of the eighth but erupted for six runs and a 9–8 win. Milt Stock was the hero in this one, getting a hit to open the inning and then the game-winning RBI single to cap the rally. With three quick outs in the top of the ninth, the Cardinals were victors, and St. Louis was atop the standings in both big leagues.

Down the stretch, the Cards would only spend five days in first place. They finished tied for third, eight games behind the Giants.

The first-place euphoria didn't carry the Cardinals or the Browns into the World Series, but the Browns came close. The 1922 season was the only one in which the Browns won more than 90 games. With 93 wins, they finished one game behind the Yankees. The Browns spent 69 days in first place and drew a franchise record 712,918 fans that season.

JESS HAINES HURLS FIRST NL CARDINALS NO-HITTER

July 17, 1924

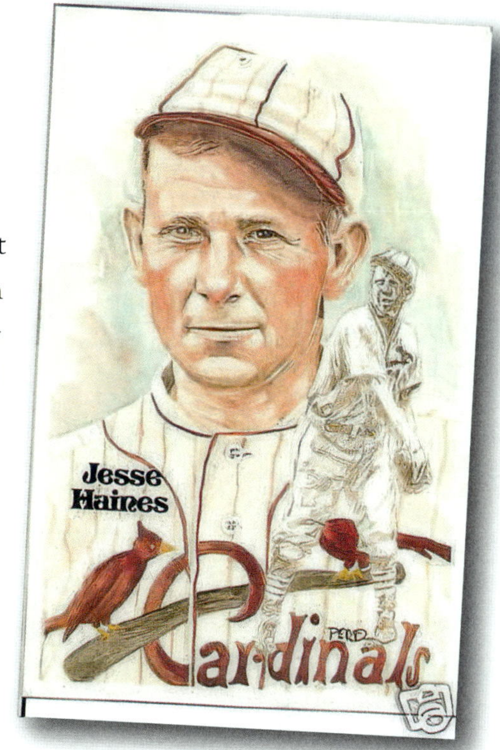

The 1924 season was a frustrating one for both the Cardinals and their pitching star, Jess Haines, as they each finished with woeful losing records. But on one shining summer day, the right-hander was unhittable, tossing the club's first nine-inning, no-hit, no-run game since the franchise had moved into the National League in 1892.

Going into the game on Thursday, July 17, the Cards were in last place, and Haines, a 20-game winner in 1923, had a record of just 5–13. But the 30-year-old veteran put on quite a performance that day before a "Tuberculosis Day" crowd of 13,000, blanking the Boston Braves 5–0.

No, the team was not giving away illnesses. Local health officials and professionals staged the event to raise public awareness of the dreaded disease and its causes and prevention. The ball club cooperated by staging a program of pregame races and competitions ranging from a "marathon" (won by one Charles Probst in 11:34) to a cow-milking contest (won by Mayor William Tiffin of Ferguson, Missouri).

In the game that followed, it was quickly obvious that Haines had his best stuff working. Throwing with his usual free and easy delivery, his fastball crackled and his curve was sharp. He finished with five strikeouts and walked three batters, including opposing pitcher Tim McNamara twice. Those were the only runners to reach base for the visitors, as the Cardinals fielded without an error. The closest thing to a Boston hit came in the second inning, when Cotton Tierney ripped a grounder toward right field. But second baseman Rogers Hornsby lunged and snared the ball with his glove and recovered his balance in time to throw the batter out at first. Haines himself knocked down a potential hit up the middle by Casey Stengel in the sixth inning. The ball rolled several feet away, but Jess got after it and retired the hitter with a rifle throw to first.

Hornsby and Haines also made big contributions on offense. The Rajah, as Hornsby was known, drove home a run in the first inning and scored one of the three Cardinals runs in the fifth. He finished the day with three of St. Louis's twelve hits. Haines himself singled and scored the Cards' second run in the third inning. Shortstop Jimmy Cooney capped the scoring with a two-out, two-run single in the fifth.

Haines breezed through the last three innings, retiring the side in order each round, and the game ended with Stengel going out on an easy grounder to Hornsby.

The victory lifted St. Louis out of the National League cellar and into a tie for sixth place, where they ultimately finished. Haines wound up with an 8–19 record.

The Cardinals have had 10 no-hitters in modern history, the last two by relative unknowns Bud Smith in 2001 (7-8 lifetime) and Jose Jimenez in 1999 (22–44 lifetime).

6 FOR 6 WITH 12 RBIs FOR BOTTOMLEY

September 16, 1924

Courtesy Missouri Historical Society, St. Louis

Jim Bottomley was the first Cardinals star to emerge from manager Branch Rickey's new farm system. A local star around his hometown of Nokomis, Illinois (near Litchfield), he had been signed by scout Charley Barrett and began his career in 1920. Nurtured through stops in the South Dakota League (Mitchell), Texas League (Houston), and International League (Syracuse), he was called up to St. Louis in August 1922 and was immediately installed behind Rogers Hornsby as the number-four hitter in Rickey's lineup.

They called him "Sunny Jim" because he made a show of how much fun he was having playing baseball. He usually sported an easy smile and always wore his cap a little off-center. In his first full season, 1923, he hit an eye-popping .371. In 1924, his average dipped to .316, but his runs scored and runs batted in increased as he adjusted to pulling the ball more out of the cleanup spot.

And no cleanup hitter ever cleaned up better than Sunny Jim did on September 16, 1924, at Ebbets Field against the Brooklyn Robins. All Sunny Jim did was get six hits in six at-bats, all with runners in scoring position. He finished with twelve runs batted in, a major league record that has only been equaled once in the nearly two hundred thousand big league games ever played. Facing five different pitchers, he had three singles, one double, and two home runs, driving in at least one run with every hit.

Although the Cardinals were mired in sixth place while the Robins were fighting for the pennant, this game was a 17–3 romp for St. Louis. Batting against lefty Rube Ehrhardt in the first inning with the bases loaded and no one out, Bottomley opened the day's scoring with a line drive single to center, good for two runs. Against Bonnie Hollingsworth in the second inning, he came up with men on first and second and two out and lashed a double down the left field line good for one run.

Bottomley did his best slugging against Art Decatur, a 10-game winner for Brooklyn that year, lifting back-to-back home runs over the right field wall. The first one came with the bases loaded in the fourth inning right after Brooklyn manager Wilbert Robinson ordered Hornsby intentionally walked to load the bases for Bottomley. The second homer came with one on in the sixth inning.

There were men on second and third when Bottomley delivered a two-run single to left against southpaw Tex Wilson in the seventh. And in the ninth against righty Jim Roberts, the slugger pulled a clean single to right to bring home a runner from third. That broke the old record of 11 RBIs in one game set against St. Louis back in 1892 by none other than Wilbert Robinson, the Brooklyn manager.

Bottomley was signed after a tryout in 1919 for $150 a month. His 12-RBI game was matched just once—by another Cardinal, Mark Whiten, in 1993.

HORNSBY REACHES .400 FOR THIRD TIME

September 27, 1925

From Tip O'Neill to Stan Musial to Albert Pujols, the Cardinals franchise has a long history of great hitters. But none topped the numbers put up by Rogers Hornsby, who led the National League in batting six times, in home runs twice, and in runs batted in four times. Those home run titles came in the same seasons as his batting and RBI titles, earning him the Triple Crown in 1922 and 1925, although the concept of the batting Triple Crown was unknown until the 1930s and not widely accepted until after World War II. He was more famous in his time for batting over .400 three times: .401 in 1922, .424 in 1924, and .403 in 1925.

Before World War I, batting average was the be-all and end-all of batting statistics, with the .400 mark setting the gold standard. The Roaring Twenties saw expanded baseball coverage in major city newspapers, including daily listings of the batting average leaders in each league for the first time. In 1921, the local papers did not agree on the official figures, and when Hornsby went hitless in the final two games of the season, the *Globe-Democrat* reported his batting average below .400, while the *Post-Dispatch* pegged his final mark at .402. Officially, he wound up at .397. In 1922, he finished with a 7-for-12 final weekend to move up from .398 to a final .401 mark. His home run total of 42 that year was well known, since it ousted Babe Ruth from the major league lead and shattered the National League record of 27, which had stood since 1884.

After an injury-riddled 1923, when he hit "only" .384 in 107 games, the Rajah rebounded with a .424 mark in 143 games in 1924.

In late September 1925, Hornsby went on a tear, rapping out eighteen hits (including three homers) in twenty-nine at-bats, boosting his average over the .400 mark for the first time since mid-August. With four games left to play, his fans were pulling for him to finish over the magic mark for the third time in five years. But in batting practice the next day, the Rajah fouled a ball off his foot, mashing his big toe and putting him on the bench for the last week of the season. The chagrined slugger admitted that some people would think he was "just gold-bricking" to protect his average, but he insisted, "I'm certainly sorry this (injury) happened because I might have got a few more home runs." As it was, he finished with a .403 batting average, 39 homers, and 143 RBIs, enough to lead all major leaguers in all three categories.

Hornsby was one of the greatest hitters of all time. His lifetime batting average (.358) is second only to Ty Cobb (.366). Many believe he was the greatest right-handed hitter in history.

CITY GOES WILD WHEN CARDINALS CLINCH THEIR FIRST NATIONAL LEAGUE PENNANT

September 24, 1926

It was Friday afternoon on September 24, 1926, when word came that the Cardinals had beaten the Giants in New York to officially clinch the National League pennant. St. Louis erupted into a wild celebration second only to the revelry seen on Armistice Day in 1918.

Like the doughboys in World War I, the Cardinals' ultimate victory came during a long journey far from home. The Redbirds had completed their home schedule on September 1 by taking four games out of five from the Pirates, overtaking Pittsburgh for first place in the process. Then they embarked on a season-ending, 24-game road trip that took them to all seven National League rivals' parks with exhibition games in Syracuse and New Haven thrown in on off days. Twice during the month, the Cards lost the lead to the Reds. They regained first place for good by taking five out of six in Philadelphia, bludgeoning Phillies pitching for 61 runs in the series. Approaching the final weekend, the Cardinals were in New York needing two more wins or two Cincinnati losses (or one of each) to clinch the pennant.

The early news Friday was good, with the Reds losing the first game of a doubleheader. In New York, however, the Giants routed Cardinals 21-game-winner Flint Rhem with a three-run first inning. But Hornsby's men launched a quick counterattack, piling up five runs in the second, two on a double by Specs Topocer, a New York native, and two on a home run by Billy Southworth, whom the Giants had traded away in June. Wee Willie Sherdel allowed New York only one run in eight innings of relief, and the Cardinals won 6–4, clinching the championship.

As the final innings were played in New York, work in St. Louis ground to a halt. Despite a heavy downpour followed by intermittent showers, large crowds gathered around radios and telegraph tickers to count down the outs. And when the game was finally won, pandemonium

Courtesy Missouri Historical Society, St. Louis

overtook the town. All business was suspended. Shredded paper confetti poured out of office windows, turning downtown streets into a sodden mass of pulp. Cars with revelers hanging out the doors jammed Washington Avenue and Olive Street, to name just a few of the centers of revelry. Fifty thousand people attending the Greater St. Louis Exposition at Fairground Park let out a collective shout when the news was announced. Telephone switchboards were overloaded with calls.

After an hour and a half, the scene quieted down as people made their way home for dinner. But in the evening, the celebration picked up again downtown, and the unbridled joy of St. Louis's first pennant in 38 years continued to flow well into the night.

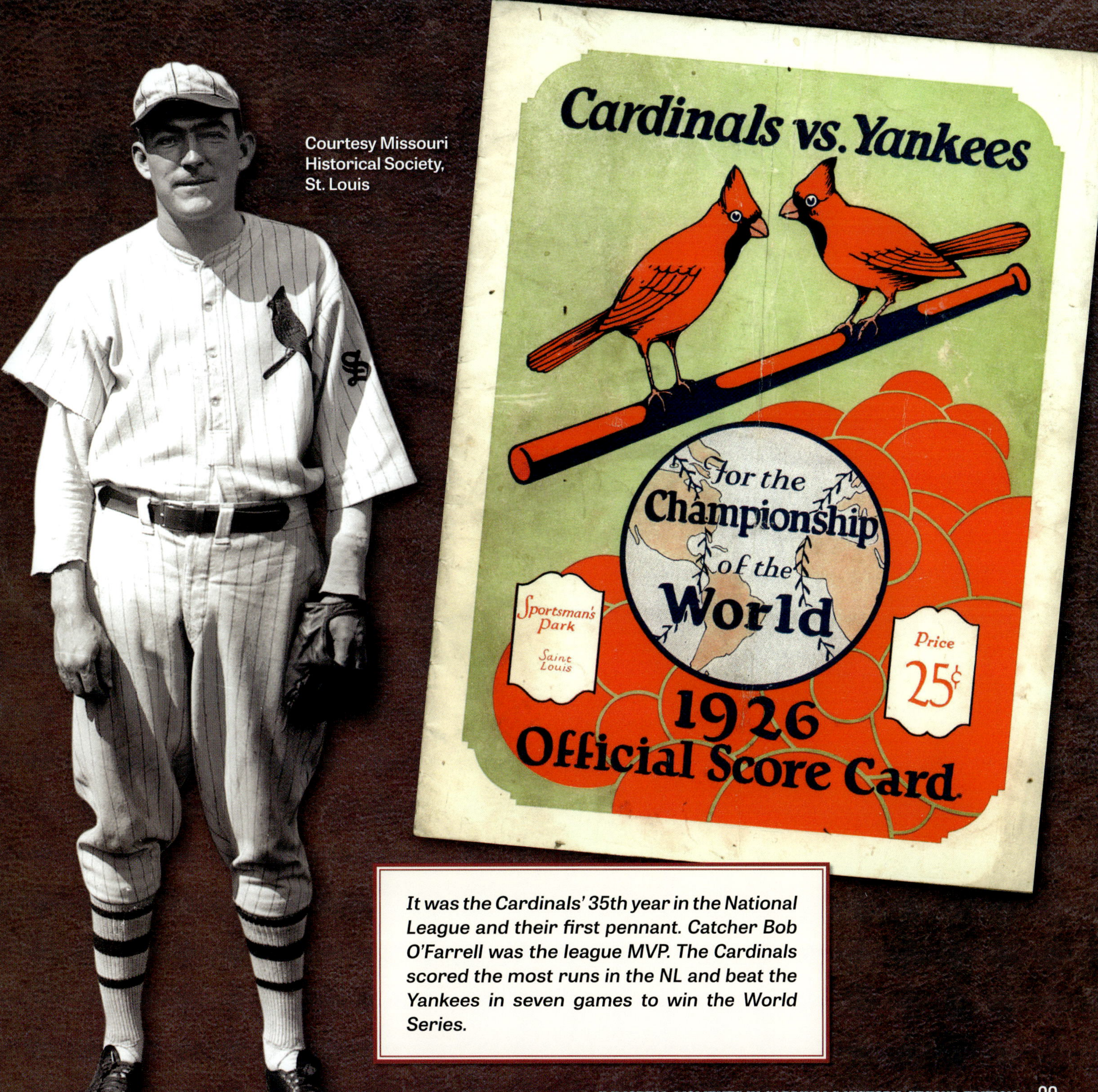

Courtesy Missouri Historical Society, St. Louis

It was the Cardinals' 35th year in the National League and their first pennant. Catcher Bob O'Farrell was the league MVP. The Cardinals scored the most runs in the NL and beat the Yankees in seven games to win the World Series.

ALEXANDER THE HERO AS CARDINALS WIN THE WORLD SERIES

October 10, 1926

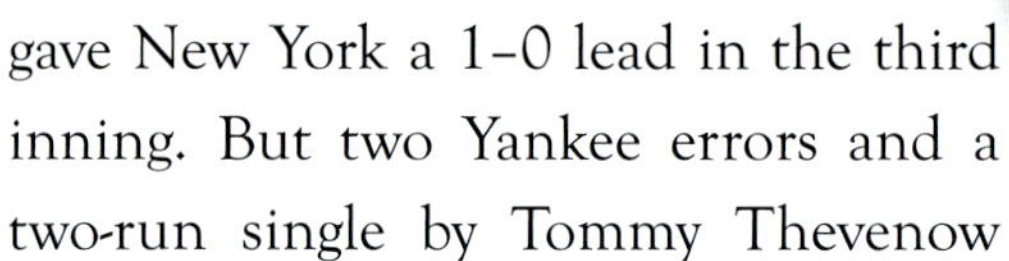
Courtesy Missouri Historical Society, St. Louis

The St. Louis Cardinals won their first World Series in 1926 with a gritty team led by player–manager Rogers Hornsby. The biggest individual hero in the series was veteran pitcher Grover Cleveland Alexander, who tossed two complete game victories and then came out of the bullpen to preserve a 3–2 lead in the decisive seventh game.

Old Pete, as the 39-year-old had come to be known, had broken into the National League in 1911 and had had a sensational career. But epilepsy and alcoholism had taken their toll, and he had won only 12 games in each of the last two seasons. His best days appeared to be behind him, and in June 1926 the Cubs placed him on waivers, allowing the Cardinals to pick him up for the bargain price of $4,000. His 9–7 record with St. Louis was nothing to brag about, but his star would shine brightly in the World Series.

After the Cardinals lost game one, Alexander got the start in the second game of the series in Yankee Stadium. Using his famous short-armed delivery and pinpoint control, he hurled a four-hitter, retiring the last 21 Yankee batters he faced as he and his teammates won 6–2 to tie the series.

Courtesy Don Korte

Alexander's next outing came in game six, also in New York. St. Louis trailed in the series three games to two, but they stayed alive with a 10–2 victory. Given a three-run lead in the first inning, Alexander allowed eight hits and two walks but was never in danger of losing the game. That evening he celebrated with a fancy dinner and perhaps a drink or two.

As the old warhorse dozed in the bullpen, Jess Haines, who had tossed a shutout in game three, pitched game seven for St. Louis. A Babe Ruth home run gave New York a 1–0 lead in the third inning. But two Yankee errors and a two-run single by Tommy Thevenow gave the Cardinals three in the fourth. New York got one run back in the sixth to cut the lead to 3–2, and then loaded the bases in the seventh with two out.

Haines had rubbed the skin off his forefinger, affecting his control, so manager Hornsby decided to bring in Alexander. Old Pete ambled in from the right field bullpen and proceeded to strike out Tony Lazzeri, although only after the rookie had lashed a long foul down the left field line. Alexander made short work of the next five Yankee hitters, but with two out in the ninth, he walked Ruth on a full count. With the dangerous Bob Meusel at the plate, Ruth tried to surprise the Cardinals by stealing second (he had stolen a base in game six, after all). But catcher Bob O'Farrell's throw to Hornsby nailed him, and the Cardinals had a 3–2 win and their first modern world championship.

"Alex the Great" was one of the best pitchers in the history of the game. A master of the curve ball, he won 373 games with an easy sidearm motion. A farm boy from Nebraska, he gained his strength husking corn. He ranked number 12 on the Sporting News list of the 100 greatest players.

FRISCH WINS THE FANS OVER

April 9, 1927

When Cardinals owner Sam Breadon announced the trade of player–manager Rogers Hornsby to the New York Giants in December 1926, St. Louis baseball fans quaked with rage. Not only was Hornsby the greatest player the club had ever had, but he had just led the Redbirds to the world championship. To send him packing seemed unconscionable.

But Hornsby's star lost some of its luster later that winter when a Louisville bookmaker filed suit against him to recover $92,000 in gambling debts. And his image was further tarnished by rancorous negotiations that lasted through spring training concerning the sale of his stock in the Cardinals ball club.

St. Louis fans also knew that the second baseman received in return, Frankie Frisch, was among the finest players in the league. The Fordham Flash, as Frisch was called, was a solid .300 hitter who had few if any peers as an aggressive runner and infielding wizard.

Frisch's very first appearance in St. Louis in a Cardinals uniform came on April 9, 1927, in the first game of the annual spring series versus the Browns. He was greeted with warm applause, but his first inning of play was a disaster. He fumbled the first ball hit to him for an error and then let a potential double-play grounder scoot right between his legs, giving the Browns two gift runs. In the bottom of the first, his woes were compounded when he grounded into a double play. But those would be just about the last mistakes Frisch made in his first month as a Redbird. He finished that game with some awe-inspiring fielding, handling 11 chances, including three double plays. And he had two hits, including a game-tying, two-out, two-run single in the eighth inning. He followed that hit by stealing second and coming around to score as the Cardinals won 5–3. Of Frisch, the *Sporting News* observed, "Fast, heady, ambitious—St. Louis likes him."

The Cards opened the regular season on the road, where Frisch fielded brilliantly and made 10 hits in 27 at-bats. When he first came to bat in the home opener, he was accorded a loud, two-minute ovation. By the end of the initial homestand, he was batting .381 with a perfect 1.000 fielding average and an outstanding total of 16 double plays in 15 games. He would continue his brilliant play all season, finishing with a .337 batting average, a league-leading 48 stolen bases, and an astonishing 641 assists, a figure that still stands as the most by any player at any position in one season. This sort of hustle and performance would make Frank Frisch a cornerstone of the Cardinals franchise for 12 years.

The trade was so unpopular that St. Louis Star sports editor Jim Gould wrote that he would never cover another Cardinals game. But Frisch won the fans over. He struck out only 10 times in 617 times at bat, stole 48 bases, and hit .337.

Courtesy Missouri Historical Society, St. Louis

CARDINALS OUTLAST GIANTS TO WIN THE PENNANT

September 30, 1928

In 1928, the Cardinals won their second National League pennant, winning 95 games to end up two games ahead of the New York Giants. The Birds led the race for most of the summer, but the Giants stayed close on their heels and actually edged ahead in late August. The critical pennant showdown featured a Thursday afternoon doubleheader on September 20 at the Polo Grounds. The twin bill drew nearly 50,000, the biggest crowd of the NL season. The teams split, with home run heroics deciding each game.

The Cardinals came to town with a two-game lead with 11 to play, and when they won the opener 8–5 behind three home runs by George Harper, their prospects improved greatly. Even though the Giants won the second game of the doubleheader 7–4 on an eighth-inning grand slam by Shanty Hogan and then took the series finale 8–5 on Saturday, they never did catch the Cardinals in the race to the wire.

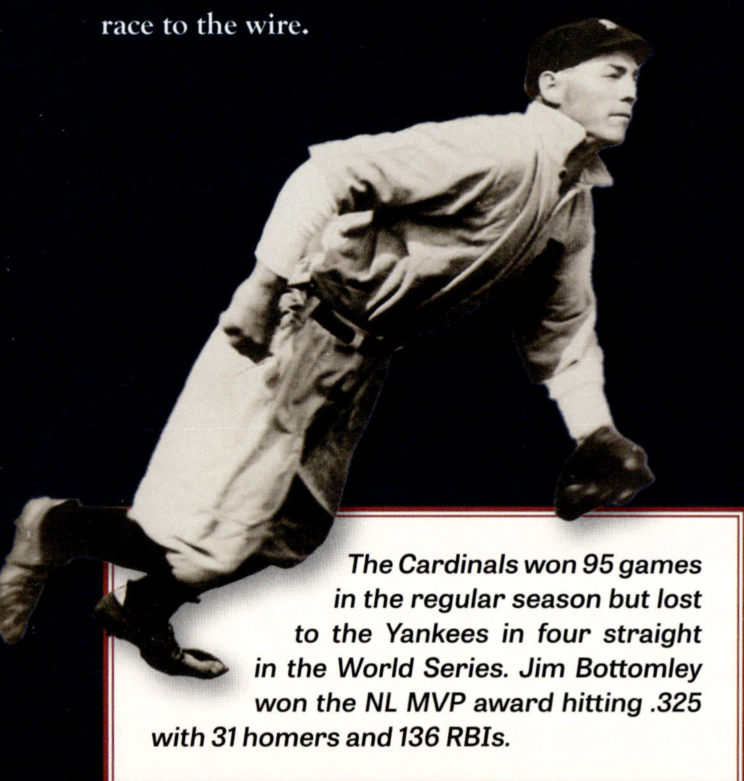

The Cardinals won 95 games in the regular season but lost to the Yankees in four straight in the World Series. Jim Bottomley won the NL MVP award hitting .325 with 31 homers and 136 RBIs.

Traded by the Giants to the Cardinals in May, Harper was a well-traveled left-handed-hitting outfielder. He would get into 99 games for St. Louis, hitting 17 homers and batting .305. His last three homers came in one critical game and made for sweet revenge against Giant manager John McGraw and the team that had traded him.

His first two home runs that game came against Larry Benton, a 24-game winner on the season. After the second homer, a three-run shot that gave St. Louis a 5–0 lead, Harper jumped on home plate with both feet while he stuck out his tongue and gave McGraw "the well-known razz." The score was 7–5 when Harper hit a long blast into the upper deck for a home run against Jack Scott in the eighth inning. Batting with the bases loaded in the ninth, Harper was called out on strikes and nearly came to blows with umpire Cy Rigler after disputing the last call.

Willie Sherdel used "his usual complement of curves and courage" in pitching the complete game for his 19th win of the season. He allowed 12 hits but no walks.

The nightcap featured ancient Grover Alexander versus rookie Carl Hubbell, and Old Pete had a 4–2 lead going into the bottom of the eighth. Then a run-scoring passed ball, a two-out error, and a 285-foot home run down the left field line beat him 7–4. In the series finale, Hubbell got another win, while Sherdel was charged with the loss, both men pitching in relief. Sherdel bounced back to win his next two starts, one a 15-inning job in Brooklyn and the other seven innings in the pennant clincher in Boston on the second-to-last day of the season.

1-0 THRILLER PUTS BIRDS INTO FIRST

September 16, 1930

The 1930 Cardinals set the franchise record by scoring 1,004 runs in the regular season and won the pennant. They scored 10 or more runs in 27 games. But their most dramatic victory was a 10-inning, 1–0 win in Brooklyn on September 16 that lifted the club into first place for good with just 11 games left to play.

The team had spent much of the summer stuck around the .500 mark, and on the morning of August 9, they were in fourth place with a 53–52 record, 12 games behind the league-leading Brooklyn Robins. By the morning of September 16, they had an 82–60 mark, just one game behind the Robins' 84–60. St. Louis had won nine of its last 11, but Brooklyn was riding an 11-game winning streak.

It was lefty Bill Hallahan's turn to start for the Birds, but he had smashed his right hand in a car door, so right-hander Flint Rhem was moved up for the assignment. Unfortunately, Rhem disappeared from the team hotel and missed the game. When he showed up later, he told a tale of being forced into a car at gunpoint and being driven to a New Jersey roadhouse, where he was forced to drink whiskey, rendering him unable to pitch. So despite a bandaged right hand, Hallahan had to pitch against Brooklyn's veteran ace Dazzy Vance in the series opener.

Both hurlers were brilliant. Vance scattered five hits and struck out 11 over the first nine innings. Hallahan retired the first 20 Brooklyn hitters before his own error (with the damaged glove hand) broke up his bid for a perfect game. He was touched for two hits in the eighth and again in the ninth, but bad Brooklyn baserunning and good St. Louis defense kept the game scoreless.

The Cards finally scored in the top of the 10th. Former Dodger Andy High led off with a pinch-hit double on an 0–2 pitch. Hallahan got a bunt down with two strikes to move High to third, and Taylor Douthit delivered a looping single to right to drive in the run.

In the last of the 10th, the Robins loaded the bases on a leadoff double followed by a walk, a sacrifice, and an intentional pass. Rookie catcher Al Lopez was the batter, and he smacked a hard shot to the left side that took a high hop. Shortstop Sparky Adams knocked it down with his bare hand, grabbed it, and zipped it to second baseman Frankie Frisch. Frisch made a lightning pivot and threw to first base for the game-ending double play. The Brooklyn players howled at the call at first base, while the delighted Cardinals skipped off the field as league leaders. They would sweep the three-game series and follow up with six more wins in their next seven games to clinch the pennant with two games to spare.

Hallahan was called "Wild Bill" for his lack of control. In 1930, he led the league in strikeouts (177) and walks (126). He was the losing pitcher in the first major league All-Star Game. He gave up a third-inning home run to Babe Ruth.

PEPPER MARTIN STEALS SERIES SPOTLIGHT

October 7, 1931

Although the 1931 Cardinals were considered by contemporaries to be the strongest National League pennant winner in decades, they were definitely underdogs in the World Series that October versus the Philadelphia Athletics. St. Louis had won 101 regular season games (the highest NL total since 1913), and the A's had won 107. It was the A's third consecutive season with more than 100 wins, establishing a major league record that has been tied but never broken in all the years since. And Connie Mack's Philadelphia juggernaut was coming off back-to-back World Series triumphs, including a six-game championship over the Cardinals in the 1930 classic.

To defeat this powerhouse, the Cardinals relied on stout pitching and superior execution on offense. Veteran hurlers Burleigh Grimes and Bill Hallahan each beat the A's twice, while center fielder Pepper Martin stole the show on offense, batting an even .500 with five runs scored, five RBIs, and five stolen bases. Little known nationally before the series, Martin's famous career as "The Wild Horse of the Osage" got its first bold notice when he became the star of the 1931 World Series.

Courtesy Don Korte

In the opening game, Martin went three for four with a run-scoring double and a stolen base against Philadelphia ace Lefty Grove. Unfortunately, the Cardinals lost 6–2. They bounced back to take Game 2, 2–0, with Hallahan outpitching George Earnshaw, who had beaten St. Louis twice in the 1930 series. Pepper scored both runs, each time after stealing a base, one run coming on a squeeze bunt by Charley Gelbert.

Martin contributed two key hits in the third game as Grimes beat Grove with a brilliant two-hitter, winning 5–2. In Game 4, Earnshaw evened the series with a two-hitter of his own, blanking St. Louis 3–0. Martin got both of the hits for the losers and stole another base.

For Game 5, Redbird manager Gabby Street shook up his lineup by moving Martin up from the sixth slot in the order to fourth, and Pepper responded with his biggest game yet. Veteran hurler Waite Hoyt retired him in the first inning, but his long fly drove home the game's first run. In the fourth, Martin beat out an infield hit but was left on base. With the score still 1–0 in the sixth inning, he launched a two-run home run into the upper deck in left field at Shibe Park. In the eighth, he had an RBI single to left to give St. Louis a 4–1 lead, on four RBIs by Pepper Martin. The bloom came off only slightly when he was finally caught stealing by beleaguered A's catcher Mickey Cochrane.

In the final two games, Martin went hitless, but he did have a key stolen base in the Cardinals' 4–2 clinching victory in Game 7.

Courtesy Missouri Historical Society, St. Louis

Johnny Leonard Roosevelt "Pepper" Martin was little known nationally before the series because he spent seven years in the minor leagues. He was an integral member of the "Gashouse Gang."

CARDINALS' EARLY ATTACK WINS GAME 7 OVER ATHLETICS, 4-2

October 10, 1931

Connie Mack's 1931 Philadelphia Athletics were one of the greatest teams in big league history, winning 107 games to capture their third consecutive American League pennant. But their quest to become the first team to win three consecutive World Series was stopped by Gabby Street's St. Louis Cardinals in a seesaw, seven-game series. In the clinching contest in St. Louis, the Cards bunched their hits in the first and third innings for a 4–0 lead. Burleigh Grimes, with last-out relief help from Bill Hallahan, made it stand up for a 4–2 victory.

Philadelphia had dispatched St. Louis in six games in the 1930 World Series, with their fastballing aces Lefty Grove and George Earnshaw each winning two games. But the 1931 series would be different, with Wild Bill Hallahan beating Earnshaw in Game 2 and Waite Hoyt in Game 5, while Grimes bested Grove in Game 3. Grimes would have four days' rest before matching up against Earnshaw in Game 7 on Saturday, October 10.

Since no tickets for Game 7 had been sold in advance, only 20,805 paid their way into Sportsman's Park for the big game. They would be on their feet

Courtesy Missouri Historical Society, St. Louis

cheering in the bottom of the first as the Cards hustled their way to two gift runs. Andy High's leadoff pop-up dropped safely when left fielder Al Simmons and shortstop Dib Williams both pulled up to avoid a collision. George Watkins's Texas Leaguer also fell just out of Simmons's reach for another single. Frank Frisch sacrificed the men into scoring position, and a wild pitch allowed High to score the first run. Pepper Martin walked and promptly stole second. With first base unoccupied, Ernie Orsatti struck out on a pitch in the dirt and dashed for first. Catcher Mickey Cochrane threw him out, but Watkins broke from third on the play, and Cochrane could not handle a low return from first baseman Jimmie Foxx as Watkins slid home safely.

High and Watkins each scored again in the third, High leading off with a line-drive single and Watkins lofting a two-run home run onto the pavilion roof in right field. Earnshaw would retire the next 15 St. Louis batters before going out for a pinch hitter in the eighth. "Old Stubblebeard" Grimes gamely held the lead at 4–0 going into the ninth, when he walked Simmons leading off. The dangerous Foxx fouled out, and Bing Miller's grounder was nearly turned into a double play. Distraught at the umpire's call at first, a fast-tiring Grimes walked the next man. Two hits followed, making the score 4–2 and knocking the gallant Grimes out of the box. With two men on base, Hallahan retired Max Bishop on a liner to center, and the Cardinals had their second world championship.

The spitball was banned in 1920, but those still using it were allowed to continue throwing the juiced-up ball. Burleigh Grimes still loaded up the ball and in two starts in the '31 series he won twice and threw seven innings of no-hit ball in Game 3.

Courtesy Missouri Historical Society, St. Louis

DIZZY STRIKES OUT 17 CUBS

July 30, 1933

Dizzy Dean was a strikeout pitcher for the Cardinals from the moment they put him into the rotation in 1932. He led the major leagues in each of his first four seasons, 1932 to 1935. On July 30, 1933, he made headlines nationwide by striking out 17 batters in a nine-inning game. The feat was hailed as "a modern record in major league baseball," and was the highest total in a big league game since 1887. Ever mindful of his audience, Dean achieved the record in front of the biggest crowd of the season, a Sportsman's Park throng of 29,500 out to see a Sunday Cardinals–Cubs doubleheader.

Aware of the power of press coverage, Jerome Herman Dean was at the time involved in a controversy concerning his actual birth date and place. It seems he had given out two different dates, in two different cities, to two different sportswriters. Eventually such prevarications would come to seem natural for Dizzy, who later was found to have been born Jay Hanna Dean at a location and date different from both of those he was claiming in 1933.

Whether he came from Arkansas or Oklahoma, or whether he was 22 or 23 years old, Dean could pitch. Working in the first game of the twin bill, he gave up a quick run on hits by the first two Cubs batters, but he struck out two to end the inning. After tossing one strikeout in the second and two in the third, Dizzy helped his cause with a leadoff double, which was followed by a single and a long fly in the bottom of the third. A quick Cub run put the Cardinals behind again, but Dean responded with five strikeouts in the fifth and sixth innings. In the last of the fifth, St. Louis rallied for five runs against Chicago starter Charley Root. Dizzy himself capped the rally with an RBI single off Burleigh Grimes. Adding insult to injury, Diz fanned Grimes to end the seventh inning. It was his 11th strikeout of the game.

With the crowd roaring, the young Cardinals right-hander poured it on in the final two innings, allowing a double but getting three swinging third strikes in the eighth inning and fanning three in row in the ninth to reach 17 strikeouts. In between, he chipped in with another RBI single, making him three for four with one run scored and two batted in for the game. His final pitch of the game was, according to Martin J. Haley of the *St. Louis Globe-Democrat*, a full-count "smoke ball through the strike zone" for a called third strike.

The Cardinals sent the big crowd home happy by winning the second game as well, 6–5. Another second-year man for St. Louis, Joe Medwick, hit a three-run home run in the nightcap to go with his four singles in the opener.

The Cardinals were the westernmost team in the majors, and in depression-ravaged America, they became "America's team" and Dizzy was a folk hero.

Courtesy Don Korte

PAUL DEAN'S NO-HITTER UPSTAGES BROTHER DIZZY

September 21, 1934

Grasping for every possible victory, the Cardinals scheduled a makeup doubleheader at Brooklyn's Ebbets Field on Friday, September 21, 1934. St. Louis was coming off back-to-back doubleheader sweeps with a couple of rainouts in between, but the Cards still trailed the New York Giants by three and a half games with just 12 to play, making every game critical. The team's top two pitchers, brothers Dizzy and Paul Dean, were both primed to pitch in Brooklyn, having started the two games of a crucial doubleheader sweep in New York on Sunday.

The Dodgers, managed by Casey Stengel and firmly planted in sixth place, gave the Cardinals little resistance in the two games, garnering only three hits. The Deans brought out a large crowd, estimated at 18,000. By the end of the second game, these Flatbush faithful were rooting for a Cardinals no-hitter. In the first game, Dizzy Dean had handcuffed the feeble Brooklyn batting order, while his teammates teed off on a variety of Brooklyn moundsmen. Dizzy had a 13–0 lead going into the bottom of the eighth. With one gone in the inning, Dodger leadoff man Ralph Boyle beat out a bouncer past the mound for the first Brooklyn hit. The Dodgers added two sharp singles in the ninth, but Dizzy was able to finish the 13–0 shutout.

The second game was much more competitive, with the game scoreless through five innings. St. Louis had only one hit, a single by Paul Dean, off Brooklyn starter Ray Benge, while Dean had set down the Dodgers on one walk and no hits. Paul put himself ahead with a run in the visitors' sixth, cracking a double to left center and scoring on a two-bagger off the left field fence by Pepper Martin. In the top of the seventh, Joe Medwick scored a run for the Cardinals, and with two out in the bottom of the inning, Medwick galloped back nearly to the bleacher wall to haul down a dangerous drive by Sam Leslie. It would turn out to be the closest bid for a hit that Brooklyn made in the game.

Paul closed out the no-hitter quickly. In the eighth, he struck out two and got a routine ground out. After an insurance run in the top of the ninth, Paul retired two pinch hitters and got leadoff man Boyle on a sharp grounder that shortstop Leo Durocher momentarily fumbled but recovered in time for the final putout. For the game, he fanned six and walked only one, Len Koenecke in the first inning. The shutout put Paul into a mythical No-Hit Hall of Fame, and it kept St. Louis's pennant hopes alive.

Courtesy Getty Images

Courtesy Missouri Historical Society, St. Louis

Courtesy Library of Congress

Brother Paul threw a no-hitter in the second game of the doubleheader after Dizzy allowed just three hits in the first game. After the game, Dizzy said, "Gee Paul, if I'd a-known you was gonna threw a no-hitter, I'd a throw'ed one too."

DIZZY'S SHUTOUT CLINCHES PENNANT ON FINAL DAY

September 30, 1934

For most of the 1934 season, Cardinals pennant hopes grew dim then dimmer. After dropping behind the New York Giants in early June, St. Louis slipped to third place and fell as far as seven and a half games behind in mid-August. With 16 games left to play (one of which was canceled), the Redbirds still trailed the Giants by five and a half games. Starting with the sweep of a Sunday doubleheader at the Polo Grounds, Frank Frisch's squad launched a 12–2 sprint to the top as Bill Terry's Giants obliged with a 5–8 slump. When the final Sunday of the season dawned on September 30, lo and behold, St. Louis held a one-game lead over New York. With a chance to be on hand to celebrate a pennant, the crowd for the finale was the largest of the regular season, 37,402.

The Cardinals needed only a victory over Cincinnati or a New York loss versus Brooklyn to clinch their fifth National League championship in the last nine seasons. The scoreboard showed an early 4–1 lead for the Giants as the eager fans were filling every inch of the grandstand, bleachers, and pavilion. The burden of victory rested squarely on the shoulders of Dizzy Dean, who was tapped as starting pitcher despite having just one day of rest after blanking the Reds on Friday. His batterymate, Bill DeLancey, gave him a 2–0 lead in the first inning with a two-out, bases-loaded single off the pavilion screen. While Dean cruised, Reds starter Silas Johnson was knocked out by three runs in the fourth inning, the RBIs coming from Leo Durocher and Pepper Martin versus reliever Benny Frey. DeLancey hit a solo homer in the fifth, his 13th of the year in just 93 games played, and he added a run-scoring single in the eighth. Jim "Rip" Collins homered with a man on in the bottom of the seventh, his 200th hit and 35th homer of the season, tying him for the league home run lead with New York's Mel Ott.

Dean cruised through eight innings without a Cincinnati runner reaching third base, while the Dodgers rallied to send the New York game into extra innings. Diz seemed to run out of gas in the ninth. A single, a double, and a walk loaded the bases with no one out. But Dean reached back and struck out the next two hitters just as news of a Dodger victory was flashed to the crowd. The roar was just building in the stands when the last Reds batter fouled out to finish a 9–0 shutout for Dean.

Euphoric fans spilled onto the field and into the streets for a long, loud celebration. Police estimated that 50,000 revelers congregated downtown and along Grand Avenue at the height of the festivities. Dizzy Dean was anointed "King of St. Louis" and the "Gashouse Gang" legend was born.

Courtesy Missouri Historical Society, St. Louis

Courtesy Getty Images

"If you done it, it ain't braggin'." Dizzy liked to boast about his ability and make predictions. Before one season he said, "me and Paul gonna win 45 games." And they did. They actually won 49.

Courtesy Don Korte

The "Gashouse Gang" nickname came from the team's generally shabby appearance. An opponent once said that the "Cardinal players went on the field in unwashed, dirty and smelly uniforms." Some accounts indicate that Leo Durocher came up with the name.

Courtesy Missouri Historical Society, St. Louis

Courtesy Don Korte

GAME SEVEN ROMP MAKES GASHOUSE GANG WORLD CHAMPIONS

October 9, 1934

Courtesy Don Korte

Twisting the Tigers' tail in Detroit, the uproarious Cardinals subdued the American League champions in the seventh game of the World Series 11–0 to bring the world championship to St. Louis. Dizzy Dean ended his incredible season by pitching a shutout on just one day's rest (matching his achievement in the pennant clincher) and getting two base hits in the third inning, when the Cardinals opened the scoring with seven runs. The triumph was partially overshadowed by a riotous outburst by the Detroit bleacher fans that nearly caused the game to be forfeited.

Dizzy Dean had beaten the Tigers in the series opener, 8–3 but had lost Game 5, 3–1. Luckily, his brother, Paul Dean, had won for St. Louis in games 3 and 6, forcing the series to the limit. There was never any question as to who would pitch for the Cardinals, but Tiger manager Mickey Cochrane was in a quandary. Having used his top two hurlers, Schoolboy Rowe and Tommy Bridges, in the previous two days, Cochrane finally decided on rookie submariner Eldon Auker, who had won Game 4 for Detroit.

There was no score when Dean batted with one out in the top of the third. He lifted a high foul that catcher Cochrane deigned not to pursue. The ball fell into the first row of box seats and might have been caught if the catcher had chased it. Diz then laced a hit to left and streaked around to second as Goose Goslin fielded the ball lackadaisically. Leadoff man Pepper Martin chopped one to first baseman Hank Greenberg and beat the play at first. Martin further flummoxed the fielders by stealing second, and a walk loaded the bases. Batting left-handed, 36-year-old player-manager Frank Frisch ripped one into the right field corner for a three-run double. With the floodgates now burst, Cochrane vainly rushed three pitchers into the breach. Dean got a second hit in the inning when he beat out a high chopper to third, as the rampaging Redbirds built a 7–0 lead.

Dizzy toyed with the Tiger hitters the rest of the way, hurling insults along with his fastballs and curves. In the top of the sixth, Joe Medwick had a scuffle with the Tiger third baseman after lacing a run-scoring triple to right center. The minor incident turned major when Medwick went to his position in the bottom of the inning. Disgruntled Detroit fans took their frustrations out on the Cardinals left fielder, tossing all manner of fruits and vegetables over the high screen in his direction, delaying the game for 20 minutes. Rather than declare the game a forfeit, Commissioner Kenesaw Mountain Landis ordered Medwick removed from the game, much to the disgust of the slugger. Fortunately, it did not matter. The Redbirds won 11–0, and Dean finished with a six-hit, no-walk shutout to make the Cardinals world champions for the third time.

Public domain

Courtesy Penale52 via Wikimedia Commons

ST. LOUIS FETES MVP MEDWICK

December 14, 1937

Any trivia maven knows that the last National Leaguer to win the Triple Crown was Joe Medwick in 1937. But in Medwick's day, "Triple Crown" was a term as yet unknown in baseball and absent from any contemporary recitation of his batting accomplishments. Joe led the league in batting average and runs batted in and tied for the lead in home runs. He also led in runs, hits, doubles, and total bases. Yet he barely won the Baseball Writers' Association of America's Most Valuable Player Award, edging Cubs catcher Gabby Harnett by a mere two points, 70 to 68. Gabby had led a late pennant charge by the Cubs and had batted .354 in 110 games played, with 12 home runs, 47 runs scored, and 82 RBIs. Joe's numbers in 154 games played were .374 with 31 homers, 111 runs, and 154 ribbies.

After the voting was announced, St. Louis was proud to stage a dinner honoring Joseph Michael Medwick, the pride of Carteret, New Jersey, which was attended by politicians, newspapermen, and baseball dignitaries from across the country. Attendance at the December 14 gala was 1,100, and the proceedings were broadcast far and wide on 60-some radio stations on the Mutual Broadcasting System.

The president of the Chamber of Commerce acted as master of ceremonies, and the editor of the *Sporting News* made the featured presentation, an engraved watch, to Medwick. The governors of Missouri and Mississippi and the mayor of St. Louis made speeches of praise, and Joe was heaped with gifts ranging from pipes to gold elephants and rabbits' feet. An avid pipe smoker, Medwick credited the proprietors of his favorite downtown shop, Jost's, for helping with his finest season. As he explained it, "One day I came in here and bought a pipe. That afternoon I hit a home run and, in fact, had a swell day all around. And after that, I noticed every time I came back and bought a pipe, I'd have a wonderful day."

Courtesy John George Medwick

Joe had many wonderful days in 1937, especially in Philadelphia. But there was one game in Philly that caused some regret. In the second game of a doubleheader on June 6, Joe hit a home run, but the home team stalled before five innings were completed, hoping to delay until the 6:00 p.m. Sunday curfew stopped play. The umpire declared the game forfeited, wiping out all the stats. As a result, Medwick finished tied with Mel Ott for first in the NL with 31 home runs, rather than leading the league outright.

The crowd at the dinner was served a fine meal—turkey with all the fixings—and a group of 16 orphans brought to the fete by the Knights of the Cauliflower Ear seemed to especially enjoy themselves. As they departed, the guest of honor and his manager, Frank Frisch, made sure that each boy went home with an autographed ball as a memento.

Batting triple crowns are rare. There have been only 15 since 1900. The Cardinals have more than any other team—four. In addition to Medwick, Tip O'Neill (1887) and Rogers Hornsby (1922, 1925) have won the coveted title. Stan Musial came close, but never won one.

MUSIAL SENSATIONAL IN SEPTEMBER TRIAL

September 21, 1941

By the end of his first week in the big leagues, Stan Musial was a star. "Nobody but nobody can be that good!" was how Cubs manager Jimmie Wilson put it after a Sunday doubleheader in St. Louis on September 21, 1941. The 20-year-old outfielder had just dismantled his team with an astonishing array of baseball talents and was already attracting attention around the wider baseball world.

Musial was the unlikeliest of phenoms to burst onto the major league scene, having ended the 1940 season as a sore-armed pitcher with three years in Class D ball. He started the 1941 season in Class C at Springfield, Missouri, where he hit .379 with 26 home runs in just 89 games played. Late in July, Musial jumped all the way up to Rochester in the International League, the top rung on the ladder in Branch Rickey's chain of more than two dozen farm teams. Musial moved right in and continued to hit, averaging .326 in 54 games with the Red Wings.

When Rochester's season ended on September 13, Musial headed home to Donora, Pennsylvania, but was soon summoned to St. Louis to help the Cardinals in a late pennant chase. Stan went two for four with a two-run double in his St. Louis debut on Tuesday, September 17, and was sporting a .500 average (six for 12) when the Cardinals began a doubleheader against the Cubs the following Sunday.

In the first game on Sunday, Stan went four for five, including two doubles off the screen in front of the right field pavilion. With two out in the fifth inning and the Cardinals down one run, he initiated a double steal from first base that resulted in Johnny Hopp sliding home safely. Musial also made a fine running catch in left field in the eighth inning. With the score tied in the bottom of the ninth, he singled with one out and moved to second on an infield out. The next batter topped one out in front of home plate and beat the catcher's throw to first. While the Cubs argued, Stan streaked around third and raced across the plate with the winning run.

Another 20-year-old rookie, southpaw Howie Pollet, was the star of the nightcap, pitching a 7–0 shutout. But Musial also made his presence felt, especially on defense, playing right field. In the third inning, he raced far to snare a sinking liner, and in the fifth he preserved the shutout by throwing a man out at home. In the eighth inning, he outdid himself with a charging, somersaulting catch. At bat, he only had two hits, one a clean shot to center and the other a bunt toward third base. His batting average stood at .545.

The Cub manager was right: nobody can be that good. But Stan Musial would be the best player in the league for years to come.

Musial's father, a Polish immigrant, wanted Stan to go to college. The University of Pittsburgh offered a basketball scholarship. His father refused to sign a baseball contract (Stan was 17). His mother finally convinced her husband to let Stan play baseball.

CARDS CLINCH FLAG WITH WINS NO. 105 & 106

September 27, 1942

Over the years, Cardinals teams have made many dramatic late charges to win the pennant. Perhaps the most incredible stretch run was made by the 1942 champions, who closed with a 44–9 rush to overcome a 10-game Brooklyn lead to gain the title. The Dodgers finished with 104 victories, but the Cardinals clinched the pennant by posting their 105th and 106th wins on the final day of the season. Their 106–48 record was the best in the National League since 1909, and their .688 winning percentage has not been surpassed by any NL team since 1942.

In the final week of the season, the Cardinals won four in a row, Monday through Thursday, to clinch at least a tie for first place. But the Dodgers did not go down without a fight, winning every game, Monday through Sunday. St. Louis was off on Friday and rained out on Saturday, so the clinching would have to wait until the season-ending doubleheader on Sunday, when the Birds hosted the Cubs.

With no radio broadcast of Sunday games, over 32,000 showed up at Sportsman's Park for the finale. Left-hander Ernie White pitched against ex-Cardinal Lon Warneke in the first game. White had been sidelined much of the summer with injuries and his record was a modest 6–5, but he had won both of his starts since rejoining the rotation. He breezed through the first three innings before yielding a run in the fourth on two hits and some daring baserunning by Cub leadoff man Stan Hack. White got that run back himself in the Cardinals fifth with an RBI single, and the Cards piled on three more runs (two on a hit by captain Terry Moore) to grab a 4–1 lead. Chicago scored a single run in the top of the seventh before White singled with one out in the bottom of the frame to launch another four-run rally. Moore knocked home an extra run in the eighth, and White set the visitors down in order in each of the last two innings to nail down the 9–2 verdict.

Courtesy Don Korte

Many observers believe that the 2004 Cardinals team was the best ever in St. Louis. But not Stan Musial. Stan the Man always felt the '42 team was the best team he ever played on. They beat the Yankees in five games in the World Series.

When the game ended and the Cardinals had clinched the pennant, the ballpark shook with joy. Jubilant teammates carried White off the field on their shoulders. In the clubhouse, the new champs were surprisingly muted until third baseman Whitey Kurowski broke the ice by yelling, "Why doesn't somebody say something? We just won the pennant." With that the hugging, kissing, backslapping, and mugging for the cameramen commenced. All the while, owner Sam Breadon worked the room congratulating each player and coach.

After half an hour of merriment, the umpires intervened to get the second game started. Backed by a second-string lineup, rookie Johnny Beazley posted his 21st win of the season, 4–1, and the Cardinals set a franchise record that still stands with 106 wins.

Branch Rickey's "farm system" was most productive. Every player on the '42 world championship team was a product of that farm system, except for one. Pitcher Harry Gumbert, who pitched just two-thirds of an inning in the series, was acquired in a trade.

CARDS STUN YANKEES IN FIVE GAMES

October 5, 1942

Coming into the 1942 World Series, the New York Yankees had won their sixth American League pennant in the last seven years and had won the world championship after each of the previous flags, losing only five games total to the National League champions in those five series. So the St. Louis Cardinals were rated as underdogs despite having won 106 regular-season games. But after spotting the Yankees the first game, Billy Southworth's Cardinals ran circles around the defending champs to win four in a row, the final three coming before record crowds in Yankee Stadium, stunning the baseball world and winning the series, four games to one.

The Cardinals had plenty of momentum coming into the series but seemed overawed in the first game. Veteran Red Ruffing held them hitless until the eighth inning and took a 7–0 lead into the ninth. Then the Redbirds came alive, scoring four runs and leaving the bases loaded when rookie Stan Musial made the last out of a 7–4 loss. In Game 2, rookie Johnny Beazley lost a 3–0 lead in the top of the eighth, but in the bottom of the frame, Enos Slaughter raced to third on a hit and an error and scored when Musial bounced a single up the middle. In the ninth, Slaughter threw out a man at third base from right field, and Beazley won 4–3.

In New York for Game 3, the Cardinals backed brilliant pitching by southpaw Ernie White with great outfield defense. And they scratched out single runs in the third and ninth innings, getting safe bunts in each rally to beat the Bronx Bombers 2–0. In the fourth inning of Game 4, Musial's bunt single ignited a six-run rally with Musial's own double down the left field line capping the scoring. A big five-run sixth by New York routed St. Louis ace Mort Cooper and tied the game at 6–6. But the Birds used three walks, a run-scoring single by Walker Cooper, and a long fly ball to push ahead 8–6 and eventually win 9–6.

In the bottom of the first inning of Game 5, Beazley gave up a leadoff home run to Phil Rizzuto. Slaughter matched that with a four-bagger off Ruffing in the top of the fourth. The score was 2–2 in the ninth before Whitey Kurowski lined a two-run home run near the left field foul pole to put the Cardinals ahead 4–2. The first two Yankees reached in the bottom of the ninth, but in a bunting situation, catcher Walker Cooper picked Joe Gordon off second to kill the rally, and Beazley closed out the series with his second complete-game victory.

After winning a torrid pennant race with 106 regular-season wins, the Cardinals steamrolled the invincible Yankees in the World Series. With the war on, there was no parade for the team, but in 1942, St. Louis saluted its greatest team ever.

Courtesy Don Korte

BASEBALL BRAWL PUT INTO PERSPECTIVE

August 1, 1943

Courtesy State Historical Society of Missouri

"Don't you know there's a war on?" was a common comment throughout the country during World War II. Whereas baseball could get contentious and downright violent, in the wider world it was and is still just a game. That was never more evident than on Sunday, August 1, 1943, when the St. Louis Cardinals hosted the Brooklyn Dodgers.

During the 1940s, there was certainly no love lost between the two clubs, and beanball battles were frequent and alarming. One of the most memorable fights occurred at Sportsman's Park during that Sunday doubleheader in 1943, which was swept by the home team in front of the largest crowd of the St. Louis regular season.

The Dodgers had strained to keep pace with the front-running Redbirds through the first half of the season, but in the two weeks prior to the big dustup they had fallen from three and a half games back to 10½ behind and had slipped into third place. So when given the opportunity to walk Stan Musial with men on second and third in the sixth inning of the first game, Brooklyn pitcher Les Webber did so by throwing first at Stan's head, and then at his ribcage. The agile young slugger, who had been Webber's target in a similar situation in July 1942, was able to avoid injury but seemed ready to charge the mound. Umpire Al Barlick stepped in front and went to the mound to warn Webber to desist, postponing fisticuffs for a few minutes.

The next batter, Cardinals catcher Walker Cooper, was still smarting from being hit by a Webber pitch in the previous inning. After exchanging pleasantries with Dodger catcher Mickey Owen, Cooper grounded out, gratuitously stepping on first baseman Augie Galan's foot as he crossed the bag. An enraged Owen raced down the line and jumped on Cooper's back as other Brooklyn players came out of the first base dugout to join in the fight. Cooper flipped Owen onto the ground and landed a few punches, while receiving a few kicks himself. Other scrapes broke out as Cardinals arrived on the scene. Police from the stands soon broke up the scuffle on the field, although the cops had more hard work to do because several fights broke out among the spectators and dozens of bottles were thrown onto the field. When it was over, Cooper and Owen were ejected and fined $50 each. Webber was docked $100 and removed, perhaps for his own safety, for a pinch hitter. The Cardinals, ahead 6–1 when the fracas started, won by a 7–1 final score and then rallied to win the nightcap, 5–4.

As the fans were leaving the park, they were confronted by news of a tragedy close to home. St. Louis mayor William Dee Becker had been among a group of 10 people killed in the crash of an aerial glider out at Lambert Field. Also among the dead was Major William B. Robertson, a retired World War I flyer who had helped found and develop the airport. He was head of Robertson Aviation, the local company that built the glider for military use. In 1944, they performed notably in the Normandy invasion. This was to be the first public demonstration of the aircraft, and a crowd of several thousand was on hand to watch. Shortly after the glider was disengaged from its tow plane, one wing fell off and the aircraft plunged to the ground, killing all aboard.

Beanballs and baseballs suddenly didn't seem like such a matter of life and death anymore.

Ten thousand people were at Lambert Field to watch the demonstration of the St. Louis–made cargo-type glider. It was flying directly over the field at about 2,000 feet when, released from the Douglas C-47 cargo plane, both wings fell off. Scores of women fainted and many in the crowd wept.

AT 91-30 THROUGH AUGUST, THE CARDS WIN THEIR EASIEST PENNANT

August 28, 1944

While the drama of the 1944 season centered around the St. Louis Browns' bid for their first pennant after 42 years of trying, for a time that summer the St. Louis Cardinals looked like they might challenge the all-time record of 116 wins. At the halfway point in the season, they were on pace to win 108 (54–23), and had an 11½-game lead. And then they got hot.

The manpower requirements for World War II affected every industry in the US, including professional baseball. Large-scale military conscription began early in 1942, and when the 1943 season opened, many big-league stars were in the army or navy, including two-thirds of the Cardinals' nonpareil outfield, Terry Moore and Enos Slaughter. Still the Cardinals, with more and better replacements available, dominated the National League in 1943 and again in '44.

In mid-July 1944, the Cards headed east on a three-week tour of six NL ballparks, where they won 18 games and lost only four. The next three weeks were played at home and the Birds did even better, going 19–3. When they began their next road trip on September 1, they held a 20-game lead, the largest in club history. Their won-lost record stood at 91–30, on pace to finish with 116 wins if they played all 154 games.

Courtesy Reedy Press

During their July-August hot streak (37–7 with one tie), they beat opponents every which way: 8–1 in shutout games, 4–1 in one-run decisions, 4–0–1 in extra innings, and 7–2 when one team scored in double digits. Catcher Walker Cooper hit seven home runs including one hot stretch when he went 15 for 19 with four homers and three doubles. Center fielder Johnny Hopp had the game-winning hit in two extra-inning victories and scored 49 runs in 43 games played. In another extra-inning affair, Stan Musial stole third and continued home with the winning run on a wild throw. Musial, playing in right, hit .348 with six home runs during the span, while first baseman Ray Sanders had 44 RBIs and a .366 average.

The pitching staff was equally dominant. Mort Cooper and Max Lanier each posted 9–1 records during the six weeks, with Lanier pitching a two-hitter and a one-hitter in back-to-back starts. Ted Wilks had consecutive three-hitters and was a perfect 8–0 despite being brained just behind the ear by a line drive in the middle of the run.

But observers were also mightily impressed with the Cardinals defense, especially shortstop Marty Marion. "Slats," as the lanky South Carolinian was called, hit seventh or eighth in the lineup but was so outstanding on defense that he won the league MVP Award.

Though the Birds won only fourteen of their final thirty-three games, they still finished at 105–49, giving the club three consecutive seasons of 105 or more regular season wins.

Somehow the Cardinals managed to field an outstanding team in 1944 despite the talent drain of World War II. Five hundred major league players served in the military sometime during the war. Marty Marion was the league MVP despite hitting just .267 with 6 home runs and 62 RBIs.

CARDINALS OVER BROWNS IN ALL—ST. LOUIS SERIES

October 9, 1944

Of all the Cardinals championships, there was one in which the triumph had a bittersweet taste at the end, the 1944 victory in the "Streetcar Series." That was the year in which the St. Louis Browns won their only American League pennant but were denied the ultimate glory of a world championship by their Sportsman's Park "roommates," the St. Louis Cardinals. The ugly duckling Browns nearly upset the regal Redbirds, getting ahead two games to one, but with superior pitching and defense the National League champs prevailed in the last three contests to take the series, four games to two.

The Brownies had won only 89 to win the AL flag by just one game. They were given little chance to topple the mighty Cardinals, who had won 105 wins and finished 14½ games ahead in the NL. Redbird ace Mort Cooper allowed only two hits in the first game, but one was a two-run homer by George McQuinn that was enough to win the game for the Browns, 2–1. The underdogs had a couple of chances to win Game 2 as well, but the Cardinals were able to eke out a 3–2 win in eleven innings. Jack Kramer tamed the Cardinals bats in Game 3, and McQuinn went three for three to pace a 6–2 win for the Browns.

Stan Musial's two-run homer in the first inning of Game 4 turned the series around, as Cardinals lefty Harry Brecheen scattered nine Browns hits and won 5–1. Mort Cooper followed with a 2–0, seven-hit shutout in Game 5.

Chet Laabs tripled and scored the first run in Game 6 for the AL champs. But a critical Brown error opened the way for a three-run Cardinals fourth inning. With men on first and third and one out, shortstop Vern Stephens's throw to second on a potential double-play ball was wide, allowing the tying run to count while getting no one out. Two-out RBI singles by Emil Verban and Max Lanier gave the Cards a 3–1 lead, which pitchers Lanier and Ted Wilks held the rest of the way. Lanier allowed only three hits but was yanked out of the game after two walks and a wild pitch in the sixth. Wilks came in and set down all eleven hitters he faced. The Browns made ten errors in the series, compared to just one for the Cardinals. Seven of the Birds' 16 runs in the series were unearned, while the Browns earned all 13 of theirs, and the Brownie batters hit a measly .183 in the series.

After losing in the 1943 World Series, the Cardinals were champions again. And even in defeat, the Browns enjoyed the season of their greatest glory.

To get to their only World Series, the Browns won 11 of their last 12 games of the season including four against the Yankees (4–1, 1–0, 2–0 and 5–2) while Detroit lost to Washington 4–1 on the last day of the season. The Browns won the pennant by one game.

Courtesy Missouri Historical Society, St. Louis

ST. LOUIS WINS FIRST-EVER PENNANT PLAYOFF

October 3, 1946

In 1946, the seesaw pennant race in the National League between St. Louis and Brooklyn ended with both teams tied with 96 wins and 58 losses, necessitating the very first pennant playoff. League rules called for a best-of-three playoff, which the Cardinals won, two games to none.

In the preseason, St. Louis was the overwhelming favorite to win the pennant, but Brooklyn led the race through much of the summer. The Cardinals nosed ahead in late August, but the Dodgers finally caught up on the final Friday of the season. Both contenders won on Saturday but lost on Sunday, preserving the tie. The playoff would begin with one game in St. Louis on Tuesday and then shift to Brooklyn for games Thursday and, if necessary, Friday.

For Game 1 in St. Louis, Cardinals manager Eddie Dyer started a 20-game winner, Howie Pollet, while Leo Durocher of the Dodgers, ever the gambler, picked a little-used 20-year-old, Ralph Branca, who was just 3–0 on the season. Everyone was aware, however, that Branca had shut out the Cards in a critical September game and that Pollet had been knocked out early in his last two starts. The Cardinals left-hander had torn a muscle in his back and had been taped around the chest and back before performing. Pollet worked very slowly, and the game took two hours and 48 minutes to complete, a long time for a low-scoring game in that era. The Cards knocked young Branca out of the box in the third inning, when they scored twice to take a 3–1 lead. In the seventh inning, three Dodger singles plated a run, but right fielder Enos Slaughter short-circuited the rally by throwing the trailing runner out at third. In the bottom of the seventh, Stan Musial led off with a triple and scored on a two-out single by Joe Garagiola. The Cardinals defense was superb, highlighted by three double-play relays by shortstop Marty Marion, and St. Louis won 4–2.

The series resumed at Ebbets Field two days later with a matchup of 14-game winners, Murry Dickson for the visitors and lefty Joe Hatten for Brooklyn. Dickson was nicked for a run in the first inning but then held the Dodgers hitless for seven innings in a row. He also put his team ahead to stay with a triple over the center fielder's head in the third inning. Enos Slaughter's two-out, two-run triple in the fifth boosted the lead to 5–1, and it was 8–1 going into the bottom of the ninth. The Dodgers mounted a desperate rally, cutting the deficit to 8–4 with the bases loaded before reliever Harry Brecheen finally got the last two men out, both on full-count strikeouts.

Although the Cardinals had been forced to go extra for the title, they were once again National League champions.

In 1946 it was a challenge just to keep the team together. Manager Billy Southworth went to the Boston Braves, joining former ace pitcher Mort Cooper. Three players jumped to Mexico for big money, and marquee players Stan Musial, Enos Slaughter, and Whitey Kurowski were all reportedly close to signing before backing off.

Courtesy of Getty Images

SLAUGHTER'S MAD DASH BRINGS WORLD CHAMPIONSHIP TO ST. LOUIS

October 15, 1946

No player personified the aggressive, hustling style of play known as "Cardinal baseball" better than Enos Slaughter. The North Carolina–born outfielder nicknamed "Country" was best known for running at top speed to and from his position every inning and racing to first even on bases on balls. Beyond the all-out style, he had outstanding talent—hitting and running, catching and throwing. His greatest season came in 1946, when he returned from three years in the army and led the National League in runs batted in with 130.

In the fourth inning of Game 5 of the World Series versus the heavily favored Boston Red Sox, Slaughter was hit in the elbow by a pitch. He promptly stole second base, but by the seventh inning, the injury had swelled menacingly, and he was taken out of the game. It was the first time all season that Slaughter was not in the Cardinals lineup. (Stan Musial played every inning in 1946.) On the long train ride from Boston to St. Louis, trainer Doc Weaver and team doctor Robert Hyland treated the elbow as best they could, but, citing the risk of permanent damage, they recommended that Slaughter sit out Game 6, at least.

With his Cardinals facing elimination in Game 6, Old Enos played despite obvious pain, contributing two walks and an RBI single to back pitcher Harry Brecheen's 4–1 win, sending the series to a deciding Game 7.

A day off set aside to sell tickets helped ease the swelling in Slaughter's elbow, and he was in the cleanup spot in the order as the Redbirds faced Boo Ferriss, the Red Sox right-hander who had shut them out in Game 3. St. Louis countered with Murry Dickson, who had lost Game 3 but had won the playoff clincher at Brooklyn. The Sox scored in the first after a bad-hop single, but Ted Williams's deep fly to center field was hauled down by center fielder Terry Moore. The Cards tied it in the third when Whitey Kurowski doubled and scored. In the top of the fourth, Williams hit another 400-foot out, this one hauled down by left fielder Harry Walker.

In the home half of the fifth, Walker bounced a hit up the middle and scored on a looping double by Dickson, a .278 hitter in the regular season. Dickson cruised home on a hard single to center by Red Schoendienst, giving St. Louis a 3–1 lead. Boston mounted a comeback in the eighth inning, opening with a single and a double to knock Dickson out of the game. Manager Eddie Dyer turned to Harry Brecheen, who had already won two games but had pitched just 48 hours earlier and was suffering from a head cold. The lefty struck out one man and got the next on a shallow fly. But Dom DiMaggio came through with a drive in the gap that sent the tying runs home. DiMaggio himself tore a hamstring racing out of the batter's box and hobbled into second. He was replaced by Leon Culberson.

Brecheen now faced Williams with the go-ahead run on second base. On the first pitch, catcher Joe Garagiola's finger was broken by a foul tip, and the drama built as Del Rice put on his catching gear and came into the game. After one strike, Williams popped out.

In the bottom of the eighth inning, Enos Slaughter stole the show. Leading off with the score tied 3–3, he smoked a single to center. Two outs later, he was still at first base when manager Eddie Dyer called for a hit-and-run play with Harry Walker at bat. Walker lined one over shortstop, and Slaughter raced around second. Center fielder Leon Culberson cut the ball off in the gap and threw to shortstop Johnny Pesky as Walker tried to stretch the hit into a double. Pesky got the ball right before Slaughter got to third base, but Country had made up his mind to score and was blazing home at full speed. He looked like a dead duck, but Pesky was caught unawares for an instant and only made a weak toss home as Slaughter slid across with the world championship run.

In the top of the ninth, Boston had men on first and third before Red Schoendienst finally corralled a bad-hop grounder to get the final out, making the Cardinals world champions for the sixth time in 21 years.

Coming all the way around from first base to home plate on a hit cut off in the gap, Cardinals star Enos Slaughter scored the decisive run in the 1946 World Series. No other single moment better illustrated the soul of Cardinals baseball, especially its first few decades of glory. And no player better personified the Cardinals style than Enos Slaughter. He hustled every moment he spent on the ballfield and was a 10-time All-Star outfielder for St. Louis from 1938 to 1953.

When Slaughter was in the minor leagues, he was walking to the dugout one day when his manager, Eddie Dyer, told him, "If you're tired, we'll try to get you some help." For the rest of his baseball career he ran everywhere he went on the field . . . including the famous mad dash in '46.

Courtesy Greg Marecek Collection

Courtesy Getty Images

SCHOENDIENST BECOMES A DOUBLES MACHINE

June 6, 1948

Albert Schoendienst, nicknamed "Red" for his orange hair and his sun-freckled complexion, was not a power hitter. He had won his spurs with good defense and savvy bat work as a leadoff man or number-two hitter. Six weeks into the 1948 season, Schoendienst's batting average had slipped to .242 with just five extra-base hits in 32 games played. Luckily, Red's road roommate, Stan Musial, was tearing up the league and keeping the Cardinals near the top of the standings.

Suddenly, in the first weekend of June, just as Stan went into his first slump of the season, Red lit up the box scores with a barrage of eight doubles in three games (all Cardinals victories). He racked up three doubles and a single on Saturday when the Redbirds outscored the Dodgers 9–6. After grounding out in the first inning, the switch-hitting Schoendienst attacked Brooklyn right-hander Harry Taylor for three straight two-baggers. In the 8th against Erv Palica, he pulled his fourth straight hit to right field, although this one was just a single. Enos Slaughter had the biggest hit of the game, a grand slam in the third inning.

On Sunday, the Cardinals switched opponents, hosting the Phillies in a doubleheader, but their second baseman did not skip a beat. Batting right-handed against southpaw Ken Heintzelman, Schoendienst doubled home the first run of the game with a shot up the gap in right center. In the second inning, he yanked a bouncer off the third baseman's glove for another double. In the fourth inning, he grounded out, snapping a six-for-six streak. In the sixth, St. Louis had four home runs, including Red's longest blast, a homer off the light tower above the pavilion roof in right field, just the fifth four-bagger in more than 450 career games. Red added another double off a different righty in the seventh inning as the Birds won the first game 11–1.

The nightcap was a much tighter affair. Facing veteran Nick Strincevich, Schoendienst drove a double off the screen in front of the pavilion in right in the first inning and bounced another two-bagger to the wall in right in the sixth. That blow was followed by a walk to Musial, an infield hit by Whitey Kurowski, and a two-run single by Nippy Jones. That was all the scoring in a 2–0 win, with Al Brazle pitching the shutout.

In a ten-for-thirteen performance in the three games on Saturday and Sunday, Red Schoendienst had one single, one home run, and eight doubles. He was at a loss to explain the extra-base power. "I'm not standing any different, I'm not swinging any harder." But for this brief moment, the ball jumped off his bat and tattooed the right field wall and screen, earning Schoendienst a niche in the record books for two-base hits.

Red hitchhiked to St. Louis for a tryout camp with virtually no money. They wanted him to stay over for a second day. He tried to sleep in Union Station but was kicked out. He wound up on a park bench until it rained. For a dime, he got a bed (full of bed bugs) in a flop house.

STAN IS "THE MAN" IN BROOKLYN

July 24, 1949

The famous "Stan the Man" nickname was coined during the 1946 season. *St. Louis Post-Dispatch* writer Bob Broeg attributed it to Brooklyn Dodgers fans, whom he surmised were chanting "Here comes the man" when Musial came to bat in Ebbets Field. And Stan certainly was The Man among opposing players in Brooklyn. In 163 games over 15 seasons, Musial batted .359 with 223 hits in Ebbets, including exactly 100 extra-base knocks. His 37 home runs in Brooklyn were easily the most by a visiting player, Ralph Kiner being second with 30.

Stan was at his peak against "the Bums" in the late forties. In 1948, in 11 games in Flatbush, Stan had 24 hits (10 singles, nine doubles, one triple, and four homers) in 46 at-bats with 16 runs scored and 13 runs batted in. With twelve walks and a hit batsman, his statistics in Brooklyn were: .522 batting average; .627 on-base percentage; and 1.022 slugging percentage. In 1949, in 12 games at Ebbets Field, his numbers were again astonishing: a batting average of .523; an on-base percentage of .633; and a slugging percentage of 1.114 on 12 singles, two doubles, three triples, six homers, 19 runs, 14 RBIs, and 13 walks. On July 24, 1949, Stan hit for the cycle for the only time in his career—in Brooklyn, naturally.

Stan had gotten off to a slow start in '49, partially because he had started out looking to hit home runs. But as the season rolled by with the Cards and Dodgers engaged in another tense pennant race, Musial began hitting more line drives to all fields. Never was that more evident than in Brooklyn on Sunday, July 24. In the first inning, Stan crashed a triple off the center field gate to drive in a run and knock Dodger starter Don Newcombe out of the game. After lefty Paul Minner retired Stan on a short fly to left center in the second inning, Musial's next three hits came against righty Carl Erskine. Musial ripped a single to right in the third, went deep over the screen in right center for a solo homer in the fifth, and doubled to left to bring home two teammates in the seventh. His four hits each went to a different segment of the outfield. Erskine walked him in the ninth, as the Cards won by a final score of 14–1.

The Cards also finished one game behind the Dodgers in the 1949 pennant race. Musial wound up runner-up in the MVP balloting to Brooklyn's Jackie Robinson and in the batting title race as well. He finished the season at .338, second to Robinson's .343.

Most consider Musial the best left-handed hitter in National League history. For all his power, he rarely struck out. He had 3,266 more at-bats than hitting guru Ted Williams with 13 fewer strikeouts (696 to 709).

Courtesy Getty Images

DEBUTS OF MOON AND ALSTON MARK CHANGING OF THE GUARD FOR CARDS

April 13, 1954

Two days before the 1954 season opener, the St. Louis Cardinals signaled their intent to rebuild their roster by trading the club's longest-serving veteran, Enos Slaughter, for three minor leaguers. The deal shocked and saddened many fans, not to mention Slaughter himself, who broke down in tears when he got the news.

On opening day, Tuesday, April 13, the Cardinals lineup featured three rookies making their major league debuts: center fielder Wally Moon, first baseman Tom Alston, and shortstop Alex Grammas. Alston, who had been purchased from San Diego after hitting a respectable .297 in the Pacific Coast League in 1953, was the first African American to play for the club. Grammas had been acquired from Cincinnati in the hopes that he would prove a worthy successor to Marty Marion at shortstop.

Although the team had reportedly paid $100,000 each for Grammas and Alston, the rookie under the most scrutiny was Moon, who had signed for a $6,000 bonus coming out of Texas A&M in 1950. Moon was replacing a man who had been a Cardinals legend and who also happened to be Moon's own favorite player as a youngster. Indeed, Moon confessed to Bob Broeg that Slaughter's famous hustling style had been the reason he had signed with St. Louis after college.

Like Slaughter, Moon was a left-handed-hitting outfielder, and he was installed in the lineup in center field, batting second. In the bottom of the first inning, Moon brought many in the crowd of 17,027 to their feet with a blast onto the roof of the right field pavilion—a home run in his very first major league at-bat. He was thrown out trying to bunt his way on in his second at-bat and later flied out twice, driving in a run with one of the outs. Unfortunately, Moon's homer in the first and a four-bagger by Stan Musial in the ninth were about all the St. Louis fans had to cheer about in the opener. The visiting Cubs routed Cardinals starter Harvey Haddix with two runs in the second and two more in the third and cruised to a 13–4 victory. Southpaw Paul Minner went the distance for Chicago, yielding only six hits and even adding a home run of his own in the top of the ninth.

Courtesy Don Korte

Neither Alston nor Grammas lived up to his billing. Moon, on the other hand, was named National League Rookie of the Year in 1954 after compiling a .304 batting average with 12 home runs and 106 runs scored. He would be named to the All-Star team twice in his 12-year career in the majors.

While Slaughter, a self-described "Southern boy," was a Hall of Fame player, it was widely known that he did not want black players in the majors. He taunted Jackie Robinson and spiked him, cutting his leg in a play at first base. He denied that he did it on purpose, saying that was typical of the way he played.

THE DAY STAN HIT FIVE HOME RUNS

May 2, 1954

Stan Musial's greatest day came in an early-season Sunday doubleheader at Sportsman's Park on May 2, 1954. In the first game, he lifted three serves onto the roof of the right field pavilion for three home runs, the last one breaking a 6–6 tie in the eighth inning. In the second game, he hit two home runs clear over the pavilion and onto Grand Avenue, giving him a new major league record of five homers in a doubleheader.

In the first game that Sunday, St. Louis faced New York's ace left-hander Johnny Antonelli, who would win 21 games and star in the World Series in 1954. Musial was walked and left on base in the first inning. In the third, Musial dropped his bat like a golf club on a low inside pitch and chipped it onto the pavilion roof to give the home team a 3–0 lead. The Giants quickly tied the count, but the Redbirds went ahead in the bottom of the fourth on an inside-the-park home run by rookie Tom Alston. With one man on in the fifth, Stan the Man made it 6–3 Cardinals with a second homer off Antonelli, another high lob onto the roof against a slow curve.

After a single in the sixth, Stan came back with his third home run of the game in the eighth inning. With two men on and the scored tied 6–6, he hit a slider from Jim Hearn to right with just enough altitude to clear the screen. The Cardinals won 10–6, and Stan was photographed happily munching a sandwich in the clubhouse between games.

In the nightcap, Stan walked and scored in the first inning. In the third, he blasted his longest shot of the day, a high drive to deep left center. But the ball stayed in the park, and Giants star Willie Mays hauled it down about 410 feet from the plate. In the fifth, against reliever Hoyt Wilhelm, he jumped on a slow one and lofted it clear over the pavilion for a two-run home run. And in the seventh he timed a Wilhelm knuckleball for another homer onto Grand Avenue, giving him five for the day. With a chance for a sixth home run in the bottom of the ninth, Musial chased a bad ball and popped out, and the Redbirds lost 9–7.

The Cardinals wound up with a split, but Stan Musial was alone atop the record book in this one category. Only one big leaguer has tied the doubleheader mark since—Nate Colbert, playing for the San Diego Padres in 1972. A St. Louis native and Vashon High School graduate, Colbert told reporters that he had been in the crowd in 1954 to witness the original five-home-run day.

Courtesy Don Korte

Courtesy State Historical Society of Missouri

The right field pavilion—310 feet down the line—was an inviting target but produced many cheap home runs. Eventually, a 21.5 foot screen was put up in front of the pavilion. That didn't bother Stan. On his five-home-run day, he hit three on the roof and two over the roof onto Grand Avenue.

Courtesy Missouri
Historical Society, St. Louis

MUSIAL'S ALL-STAR-GAME-WINNING HOMER

July 12, 1955

Stan Musial was an all-star major league all-star. Stan the Man holds at least a share of the record for most All-Star Games played (24) and most home runs (six) and extra-base hits (eight). He first became the leader in appearances in the 1955 game, played in Milwaukee, when Stan played in his 12th Midsummer Classic. Though he started the game on the bench and was hitless in his first three at-bats, Musial made the 1955 game his most memorable with a walk-off home run in the bottom of the 12th inning, giving the National League a 6–5 victory.

Having been named to the starting lineup in 10 of the 11 All-Star Games from 1943 to 1954, Stan was a substitute in 1955 for only the second time in his career. He was playing first base that season and finished behind the Reds' Ted Kluszewski in the fan balloting. Having led the league in homers and RBIs in 1954, Big Klu was leading in long balls again with 29 at the All-Star break in 1955, while batting .317 with 65 RBIs. Musial's stats were 17 homers, 65 RBIs, and a .298 average.

Kluszewski's prowess notwithstanding, National League skipper Leo Durocher did not wait long to get Musial into the game. After the mandatory three innings expired for the starters, Stan was inserted as a pinch hitter for left fielder Del Ennis in the fourth inning and the NL down 4–0. Musial struck out but stayed in the game. In the sixth inning, he bounced into a double play, and in the seventh, he tapped weakly to second base. The National League bounced back to tie the score, 5–5, nonetheless. Musial was walked and left on base in the ninth.

The game dragged into extra innings. Scheduled to lead off the bottom of the twelfth, Stan moaned, "They don't pay us to play overtime." Then he launched the first pitch, an inside fastball from right-hander Frank Sullivan, on a high arc to right field, a "no doubt" home run over the wire fence. Sullivan glumly trudged off the mound, while Musial sailed around the bases to a hero's welcome. It was his All-Star Game-record fourth homer, breaking a tie with Ted Williams and Ralph Kiner. Previously, Stan had poled four-baggers against Walt Masterson in 1948 in St. Louis, off Mel Parnell in 1949 in Brooklyn, and versus Eddie Lopat in Detroit in 1951. He would add two more: against Tom Brewer in 1956 in Washington and off Gerry Staley in 1960 in Yankee Stadium.

Even among the very best stars, Stan Musial was an all-star.

There have been just three walk-off home runs in the major league All-Star Game. Ted Williams did it in 1941, and Johnny Collison of the Phillies accomplished the feat in the 1964 game. And, of course, Musial hit the first pitch in the 12th inning in the National League win in 1955.

VON McDANIEL ELECTRIFIED ST. LOUIS IN HIS FIRST START

June 21, 1957

Just a month out of high school, 18-year-old pitcher Von McDaniel captivated the home crowd in his first start for St. Louis, beating the defending league champion Brooklyn Dodgers in a tension-packed game. With the score 0–0 in the sixth inning, the teenager coolly pitched out of a bases-loaded, no-out jam, earning his first standing ovation of the night. He would get a couple of more ovations as he nailed down the victory, 2–0.

A "bonus baby," just like his brother Lindy, Von McDaniel signed a $50,000 contract right after graduating from high school in Hollis, Oklahoma. His first game action was four scoreless innings of mop-up relief on June 13. Three days later, he picked up his first win with another four shutout innings against the Dodgers in Brooklyn. Over those first eight innings of pitching, he allowed just two hits and no walks.

Although it was not announced ahead of time, Von was given the ball to start the opener of a home series against the Dodgers on Friday night, June 21. He was matched up against another rookie, 24-year-old left-hander Danny McDevitt, who had pitched a complete game win in Cincinnati in his big-league debut just four days earlier. Both youngsters were dominant early, and five scoreless innings went on the board quickly. Jim Gilliam led off the Dodger sixth with a looper that just eluded second baseman Don Blasingame's leaping attempt for the first hit off McDaniel. Pee Wee Reese bunted, and both runners were safe when first baseman Stan Musial dropped the ball. Duke Snider tried another bunt, and this one rolled past the mound for a hit, loading the bases. With his brother squirming on the bench and 27,000 fans holding their collective breath, McDaniel calmly induced Elmer Valo to hit a comebacker, which he converted into a one–two–three double play. Then, with Reese bluffing starts off third base, the young righty got Gino Cimoli to tap back to the box for the third out. The crowd burst into cheers and rose to give McDaniel a big hand as he walked off the mound.

The Cardinals broke through against McDevitt in the bottom of the sixth with two walks, Musial's first sacrifice bunt of the season, and a run-scoring bouncer by Del Ennis. McDaniel pitched a perfect seventh and worked around a leadoff walk in the eighth before receiving another standing ovation in the bottom of the eighth. He flied out against reliever Don Bessent, but Blasingame followed with a triple and came home on a single by Alvin Dark. With a 2–0 lead, the unflappable rookie had a quick ninth to finish with a two-hit shutout and earn another long ovation from the crowd.

McDaniel's meteoric rise in 1957 was followed by a meteoric crash the next year because of inexplicable wildness on the mound. His career record was seven wins and five losses. Attempts to come back as a third baseman failed. McDaniel died at age 56 of a heart attack.

Courtesy Getty Images

Courtesy Getty Images

Stan is the only player to get hit number 3,000 as a pinch hitter. He was the first one in 16 years to accomplish the feat. There were 5,692 on hand at Wrigley that day.

Courtesy Greg Marecek Collection

HIT NO. 3,000 FOR MUSIAL

May 13, 1958

When the 1958 season began, everyone knew it was only a matter of time before Stan Musial entered the exalted 3,000-hit club. He had won his seventh batting title in 1957 and stood just 43 hits shy of 3,000 at the start of the 1958 season. Stan attacked the milestone with gusto, blistering 41 hits in the first 21 games of the season, putting him at 2,998 when the Cardinals traveled to Chicago for a quick, two-game road trip. When Stan smacked a double in four at-bats in the Monday game at Wrigley, manager Fred Hutchinson announced that he would be benched in the Tuesday finale, so that he could get number 3,000 back in St. Louis. Hutchinson added the important caveat that Musial might be used as a pinch hitter in the game in Wrigley.

Getting his first game off of the season, Stan spent the early innings on May 13 sunning himself in the Cardinals bullpen while watching the Cubs get out on top of a 3–1 lead against Redbird starter Sam Jones. When the pitcher's spot in the order came up in the visitors' fifth, there was one on and one out, and Hutchinson summoned Musial in to bat.

The lazy afternoon suddenly became electric with anticipation as Stan picked out a bat and went to the plate. First base was open, allowing Cub right-hander Moe Drabowsky to work carefully, though Musial represented the tying run. With the count two and two, Drabowsky tried to spot a curveball on the outside corner. The pitch was just a little bit higher than he had hoped. Uncoiling from his stance in the back corner of the batter's box, Stan strode into the pitch. Keeping his hands back, he pivoted his hips into the swing and then drove the bat through the strike zone. The result was a long liner down the left field line, hit number three thousand.

Stan cruised into second base with a standup double, and the celebration began. Third base umpire Frank Dascoli got the ball and presented it to The Man, beaming at second base. Manager Hutchinson ran out of the dugout to congratulate his star, followed by a raft of photographers. A pinch runner, Frank Barnes, took Musial's place on second base, and the great one and most of the reporters headed for the clubhouse. Stan stopped on the way to kiss his wife, Lillian, who was watching from a front-row seat. While Musial fielded questions in the clubhouse, the Cardinals parlayed Stan's big hit into a four-run rally that won the game 5–3.

On the train trip home, Stan made impromptu speeches to crowds at the stations in Springfield and back in St. Louis, where more than 1,000 people gathered to greet him late at night. "Now I know how Lindbergh felt," Stan quipped. A fan yelled back, "You're greater than Lindbergh, Stan." The whole throng agreed.

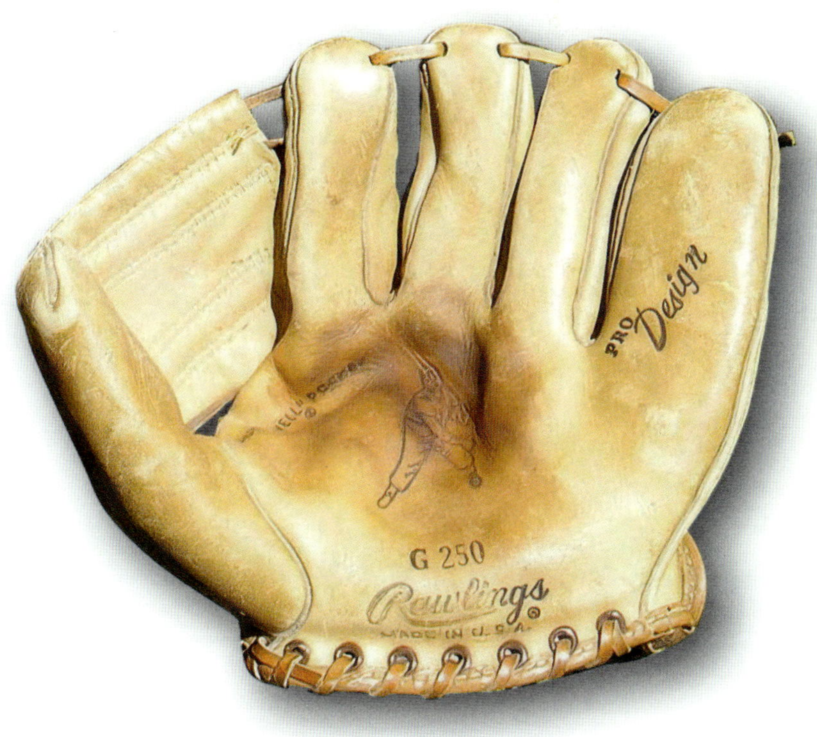

THE MAN HOMERS IN FOUR STRAIGHT AT-BATS

July 8, 1962

By 1962, Stan Musial had become the grand old man of the National League. Forty-one years of age at the start of the season, he was the oldest position player in the league, nearly two years older than the two 39-year-olds on NL rosters, Minnie Minoso and Red Schoendienst. Stan had marched through a host of milestones in the previous few seasons, but his batting average had fallen well below .300 for three years in a row. Somehow in 1962, he roused his shillelagh for one more big season, finishing a close third in the batting race with a .330 mark while collecting 19 homers among his 143 total hits and knocking in 82 runs.

One reason cited for his dramatic improvement was the expansion of the league from eight to 10 teams. Against the woeful 1962 Mets pitchers, Musial batted a nifty .468 with four home runs among his 22 hits. All four of those homers came in consecutive official at-bats over two days in July. Stan had been in a slump, and after going hitless in the series opener against the Mets on Friday, his average had plummeted from a league-leading .347 to .317 in 10 days. Saturday featured a twi-night doubleheader, with Stan sitting out the opener except for a successful pinch-hitting appearance. In the nightcap, he had a single in the fourth inning and a tie-breaking home run in the eighth inning of a 3–2 win. It was The Man's 46th home run at the Polo Grounds, 18 more than any other visiting player on that site.

On Sunday, July 8, he followed up that round-tripper with three more home runs in his first three official at-bats. Against Met starter Jay Hook, Stan homered in the first inning, walked in the third, and homered again in the fourth. Both blows were drives into the upper deck in right. In the seventh, Musial faced lefty Willard Hunter and tomahawked a high fastball up against the facing of the roof in right, his third of the day and fourth in a row (not counting the walk). Trying for a homer in the eighth, Stan chased a wild pitch from old teammate Bob Miller and struck out, though he made it to first base safely. He was replaced by a pinch runner.

With Bob Gibson pitching a three-hitter (and smacking a home run of his own), the Redbirds won easily, 15–1. In fact, by tacking on three runs in the ninth, Musial's number-four spot in the batting order came up again, meaning Stan would have gotten a shot at another home run. The missed opportunity notwithstanding, no one was complaining about Stan the Man's performance.

Courtesy Missouri Historical Society, St. Louis

The feat has been done just 16 times in MLB history. Other notables who have hit four home runs in four at-bats include Albert Pujols, Mickey Mantle, and Bo Jackson.

Courtesy Don Korte

CARDS WIN 19 OF 20 TO LEAP INTO CONTENTION

September 15, 1963

With one of the most dramatic hot streaks in club history, 19 wins in 20 games, the 1963 Cardinals leaped into pennant contention in the final month of the season. Although the Redbirds failed to win the pennant, the spurt captivated the local consciousness and provided a harbinger of the team's historic run to the pennant in 1964.

The Cards were in third place, seven games behind the Dodgers, when the streak began on August 30 in Philadelphia. The turnaround began with a three-game sweep of the Phillies, with Ken Boyer homering for the Cardinals in each game. Back at home against the Pirates, the Birds took both games of a Labor Day doubleheader as part of another three-game sweep. Two quick wins over the Mets followed. Boyer delivered the tie-breaking run in the opener to reach 100 RBIs for the first time in his career, while Curt Flood went five for five and Curt Simmons pitched a shutout in the second game. Simmons would have three shutouts among his four complete-game wins during the hot streak.

At Pittsburgh, Bob Gibson ran the Cardinals winning streak to nine games in the first game of a Friday night twin bill. In four starts during the 20-game stretch, Gibson allowed only four runs in 35 innings pitched, while driving in six runs in 13 at-bats. In the Friday nightcap, however, Pirate lefty Bob Veale blanked the Birds, 5–0. The setback left St. Louis five and a half games behind Los Angeles with 20 to play.

The Cards bounced back with tense, one-run victories on Saturday and Sunday. The Dodgers, meanwhile, lost two in a row. When the Cardinals flew home, they were trailing by 3 and a half games, and a crowd of several thousand greeted them at the airport.

A four-game sweep of the Cubs, Monday through Thursday, made pennant fever even hotter. Three of the wins were shutouts. On Tuesday, Stan Musial delivered a home run in his first at-bat after learning of the birth of his first grandchild. On Wednesday, St. Louis–boy Mike Shannon hit his first major league home run. Friday to Sunday saw another four-game sweep, this one with the Braves as the victims. Venerable Warren Spahn was knocked out early on Friday, while Simmons cruised to his third consecutive shutout. On Saturday, Gibson got the win, though Ron Taylor had to pitch out of a two-on, no-out jam in the ninth to preserve the 3–2 decision. Sunday's doubleheader drew over 30,000, who saw another 3–2 nailbiter, followed by a 5–0 shutout by Ray Sadecki.

The ten-game winning streak put the Cardinals (91–61) just one game behind the 91–59 Dodgers, who came to town on Monday, September 16. But St. Louis's bubble burst, as Los Angeles swept three games to virtually end the pennant race.

The strength of the team in 1963 lay in the infield of Ken Boyer, Dick Groat, Julian Javier, and Bill White. All four were starters for the National League in the All-Star Game that summer. Only one other team has ever had its whole infield start in the Mid-Summer Classic, the 2016 Cubs.

Courtesy Getty Images

It was ironic that Musial's last hit went past Cincinnati rookie second baseman Pete Rose, who would eventually pass Stan in career hits. It was his 1,815th hit at home. He also had 1,815 hits on the road.

"WE WON'T BE SEEING HIS LIKE AGAIN"–STAN'S LAST GAME

September 29, 1963

The most fabled playing career in St. Louis sports finally came to an end on the last Sunday of the 1963 season. Since the announcement on August 12 that he would retire, Stan "The Man" Musial had been feted and fawned over in every National League city the Cardinals visited. Club presidents and mayors across the land plied Musial with plaques and proclamations. Umpires and opposing players were unashamedly effusive in their admiration.

Finally, on the last day of the season, it was St. Louis's turn. The crush of media was handled as only Stanley Musial could. This was his party, and at one point when the nostalgia became a bit oppressive, Stan scolded, "Snap out of it, this is a happy occasion." Photographers and reporters were with him when he woke up, with Stan and Lil and their family at mass at St. Raphael's, and back at home for breakfast. Three cameramen were crammed into the back seat of his Cadillac as he drove to the ballpark.

He walked into the Cardinals clubhouse at 10:50 a.m. His heart may have hung heavy, but he joked with the mass of cameramen, "I've changed my mind, I'm not retiring." Teammates old and new came by to pay respects and collect autographs. In batting practice, old teammate Lloyd Merritt finally served one up just right, and Stan wowed the crowd with a drive onto the pavilion roof.

There were more than 30 minutes of speeches before the game, emceed by Harry Caray and featuring baseball and civic leaders and newspapermen Bob Broeg and Bob Burnes. Last on the program was The Man himself. He began his speech, "With humble pride, thanks to everyone." He also thanked "God for giving me the talents and good health to make these 22 years possible."

Facing flamethrower Jim Maloney in the final game, Stan struck out in the first inning. In the third, he lined one to center, between the bag and the diving second baseman, rookie Pete Rose. In the sixth inning, he came up with a runner on second. Up in the broadcast booth, Caray admonished his audience to "take a good look, the stance, the swing, we won't be seeing his like again." Picking out a low-and-inside pitch, he smacked it on the ground to right field for another single. As the crowd roared, Curt Flood motored home with the first run of the game.

A pinch runner took Musial's place on base, and there were very few dry eyes in the park as Stan kissed his wife and repaired to the clubhouse with most of the reporters and cameramen. The queries and musings continued inside, while outside the game dragged into extra innings. At last, the Cardinals won in the fourteenth, 3–2, and Stan could finally appear on the star of the game show before leaving the park around 7:45. "When he left," as Lowell Reidenbaugh of the *Sporting News* put it, "an era left with him."

Courtesy Don Korte

CARDS CLINCH ON THE FINAL DAY

October 4, 1964

In winning the Cardinals' first pennant in 18 years, the 1964 Cardinals took a chapter from the past and made a breathtaking rush to capture the flag by winning the last game of the season. Reminiscent of the 1934 and 1942 champs, this year's team overcame a seemingly insurmountable deficit to snatch the lead in the final week, clinching the championship on the final Sunday. All those clinchers came in front of ecstatic home crowds. The 1964 pennant would be the last one at the revered Grand Avenue ballpark, which was named Busch Stadium from 1953 until 1966 but was known as Sportsman's Park to older generations.

In the preseason, the Cardinals were rated as potential contenders in 1964, but they were under .500 as late as July 24, tied for seventh place. Three weeks later, they were up to fourth place but 11 games behind the first-place Phillies, a season high. They pushed into second place by Labor Day. But with just two weeks to go (13 games left to play), St. Louis was still tied for second with Cincinnati, and both trailed Philadelphia by six and a half games. St. Louis stayed alive by sweeping five games in Pittsburgh while Philadelphia folded, going 0–7 against the Reds and Braves. Back in St. Louis, the Cardinals steamrolled the Phillies, never trailing during a three-game sweep. Suddenly the Redbirds had a half-game lead over the Reds with just one series to go. The Cards had won eight in a row and were due to finish against the cellar-dwelling Mets, losers of eight straight.

In mid-August, Cardinals owner Gussie Busch, figuring the Cardinals were out of the race, fired general manager Bing Devine. He also made a verbal offer to Leo Durocher to manage the team in 1965. But the team stunned Busch and the baseball world by rallying and winning the pennant and World Series.

The Friday night game jolted St. Louis, with lefty Alvin Jackson edging Bob Gibson as the Mets won 1–0. On Saturday, the Cards made five errors and were embarrassed 15–5. When the final day dawned, the Cardinals were tied with the Reds. The Phillies could still get into a three-way playoff by beating Cincinnati if New York beat St. Louis again.

A full house of 30,147 fans showed up at Busch Stadium on Sunday, and the news on the scoreboard was good—Philadelphia grabbing an early 3–0 lead in Cincy and pulling away for a 10-0 win. In St. Louis, the home team got out to leads of 1–0 and 2–1 before the Mets went ahead 3–2 in the middle of the fifth. Bob Gibson was brought in to replace starter Curt Simmons, and he quelled the rally. In the bottom half, the Redbirds regained the lead with three runs, Ken Boyer contributing a key double. Three Cardinals runs in the sixth and three more in the eighth put the game away, although Gibson ran out of gas in the ninth and knuckleballer Barney Shultz finished up. The final score was 11–5, and Gussie Busch, sitting in the owner's box next to the dugout, finally got to celebrate his first pennant in his 12th year of trying.

Courtesy Don Korte

Courtesy Missouri Historical Society, St. Louis
NYLON
Stitched
SEARS, ROEBUCK AND CO. U.S.A.

Courtesy Missouri Historical Society, St. Louis

Courtesy State Historical Society of Missouri

CARDINALS OUTLAST YANKEES IN GAME 7 TO WIN WORLD SERIES

October 15, 1964

Adding another chapter to their long list of unlikely titles, the St. Louis Cardinals won the franchise's seventh world championship by beating the New York Yankees in a dramatic, seven-game series. The clincher featured the third matchup between Cardinals ace Bob Gibson and Yankee rookie Mel Stottlemyre. They had split their previous starts, but Stottlemyre was knocked out of Game 7 early, while Gibson, despite laboring at the end, went the distance for a 7–5 victory and St. Louis's first world championship in 18 years.

The series had seesawed back and forth. St. Louis won the opener before New York took the next two games, one on a walk-off home run by Mickey Mantle. Dramatic home runs by Ken Boyer and Tim McCarver won the next two contests for the Cardinals. But the Yankees tied the series by winning Game 6 in St. Louis.

Both starting pitchers for Game 7 were working on just two days' rest. Both got through three innings without allowing a run. In the bottom of the fourth, however, Stottlemyre, trying to complete a three-six-one double play, could not corral shortstop Phil Linz's errant throw, allowing Boyer to score the game's first run. McCarver later scored on a double steal executed with Mike Shannon; and Shannon himself came home on a hit by Dal Maxvill,

In a bizarre twist, the Yankees fired manager Yogi Berra after the series. Cardinals manager Johnny Keane resigned from the Cardinals and was hired by the Yankees as their new manager, replacing Berra.

Courtesy Don Korte

upping the St. Louis lead to 3–0. With Stottlemyre removed for a pinch hitter, the Cards added three more runs in the fifth against Al Downing, starting with a leadoff homer by Lou Brock.

The euphoria of a 6–0 lead lasted only briefly, as Mantle drove an opposite-field, three-run homer into the bleachers with none out in the sixth. Manager Johnny Keane paid a visit to the mound but left his big man in, and Gibson got through the sixth, seventh, and eighth without any more serious threats. Boyer added a solo homer in the home seventh, building the Redbird lead to 7–3.

In the ninth, Gibson fanned the leadoff hitter on a foul tip, but Clete Boyer (Ken's brother) connected for a home run of his own. After another foul tip strikeout, Phil Linz whacked the inning's second home run, cutting the lead to 7–5. Keane went to the mound again, and again he left Gibson in. Bobby Richardson, with 13 hits already in the series, finally ended it with a weak pop out to second base.

The Cardinals were world champs! Gibson collapsed into Boyer's arms on the mound as fans streamed onto the field. In the clubhouse, a wild celebration ensued, featuring champagne and shaving cream, while the city partied well into the night.

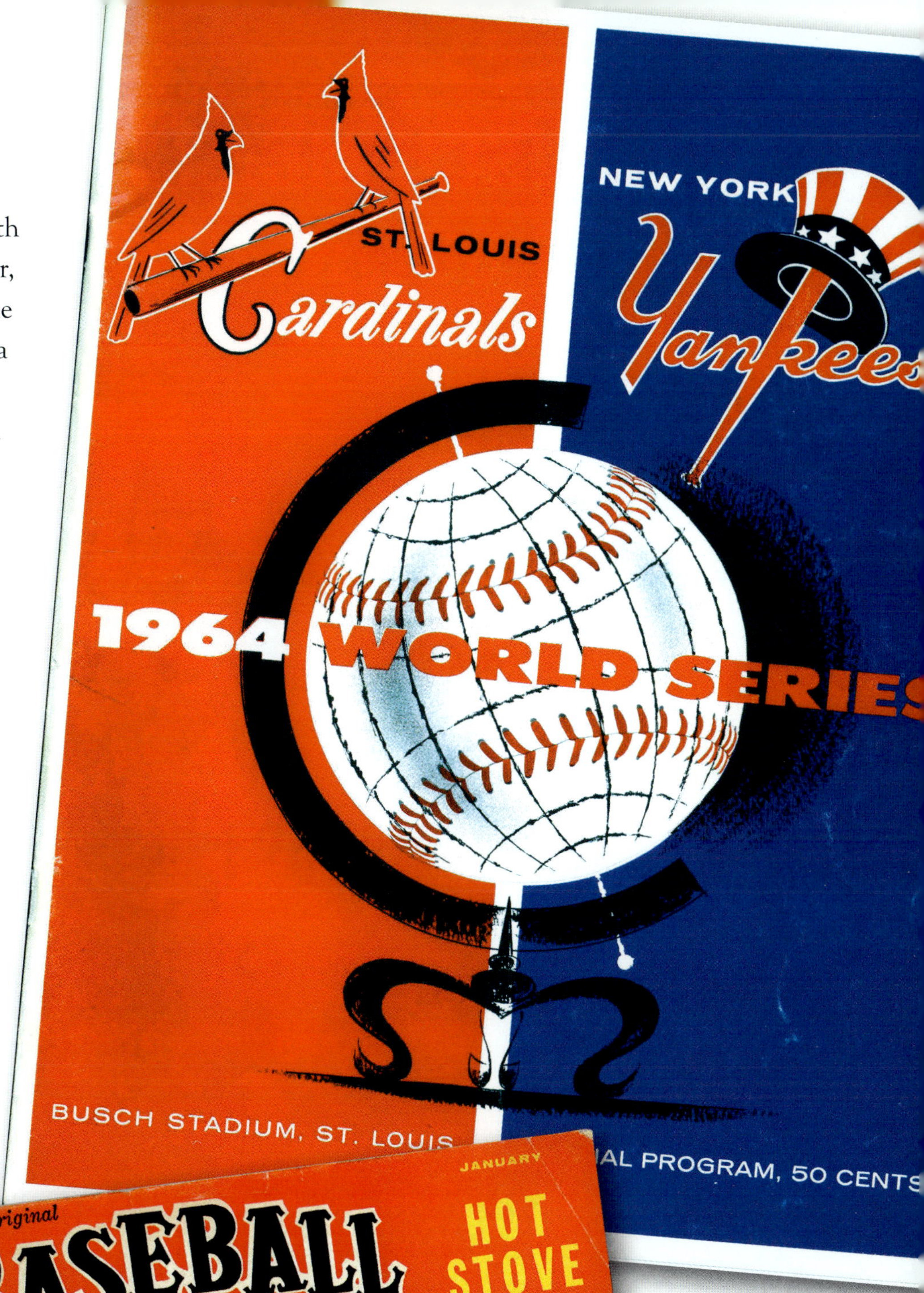

Courtesy Missouri Historical Society, St. Louis

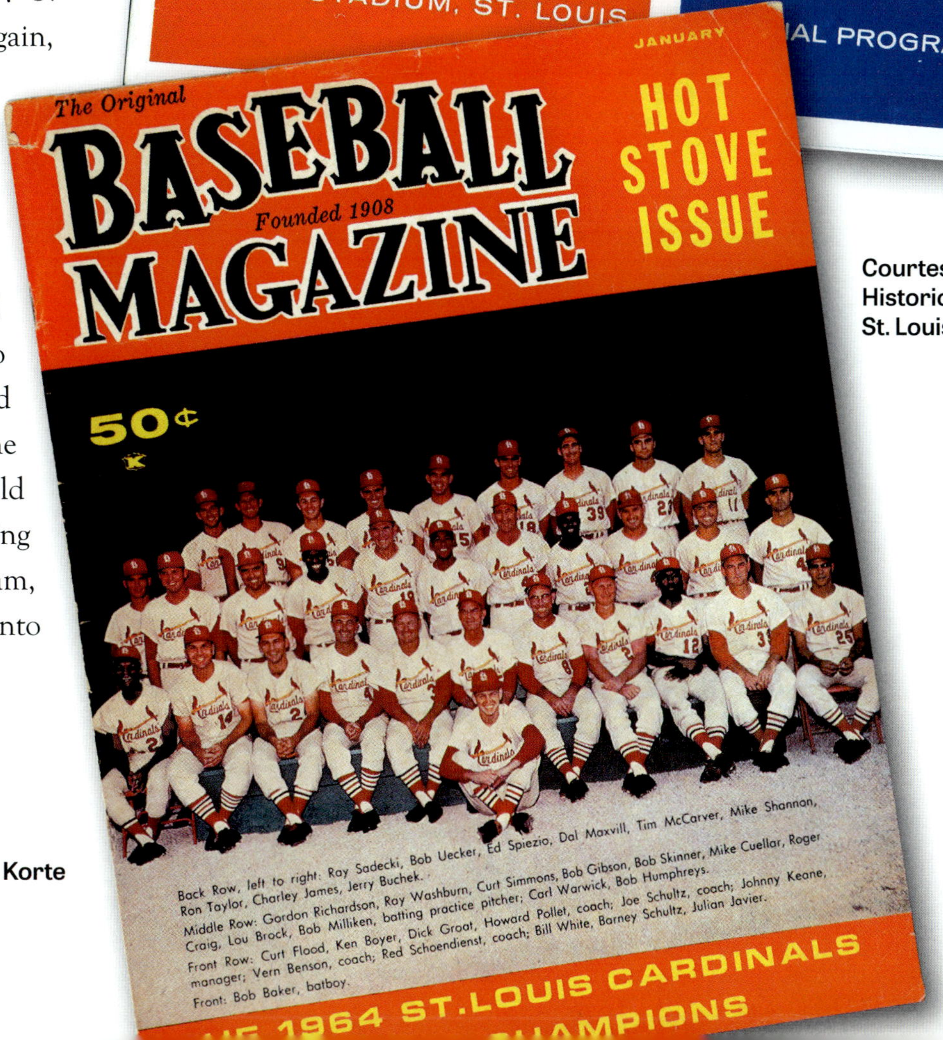

Courtesy Don Korte

NEW BUSCH MEMORIAL STADIUM OPENED DOWNTOWN

May 12, 1966

A new era in St. Louis baseball dawned in May 1966 when the Cardinals opened an expansive new ballpark downtown. Officially titled Civic Center Busch Memorial Stadium (and commonly called Busch Memorial Stadium until 1982, when the "Memorial" was dropped), the new stadium was designed to house both the baseball Cardinals and the professional football Cardinals. With a seating capacity listed as 49,450, it could accommodate nearly 19,000 more than the old Busch Stadium (formerly Sportsman's Park) that it was replacing. Built for around $26 million by the Civic Center Redevelopment Corporation, a consortium of area companies and labor unions, it was named after Anheuser–Busch, Inc., the company that owned the baseball club and also the single largest contributor ($5 million) to the project.

Originally planned to be ready for the opening of the 1966 season, late delivery of some of the structural steel and labor problems forced the opening date back to May 12. The park was still not quite finished when that date arrived, but an enthusiastic crowd poured out of the adjacent parking garages and the downtown streets early to take a good look around. The natural gas connections were not completed, so there was no hot food at the concession stands, and the mechanical tarp that was supposed to cover the infield was not quite functional yet. Recent rains made the field soggy, and unseasonably chilly weather made the patrons long for warmer fare than peanuts and beer.

But all in all, the park drew favorable reviews. In contrast to the old Sportsman's Park, everything was commodious, from the walkways and concession areas to the playing field itself. The new park had an arcing, nearly circular boundary, substantially increasing the home run distances.

After opening ceremonies, a long parade of dignitaries followed owner August A. Busch Jr. up to the glassed-in Stadium Club for a catered party,

Courtesy Missouri Historical Society, St. Louis

and the game began, with Ray Washburn pitching for the Cardinals against Wade Blasingame and the Atlanta Braves. A Brave got the first hit, but St. Louis natives Jerry Buchek and Mike Shannon scored the first runs, Shannon tripling home Buchek and then scoring on a hit by Curt Flood. Atlanta leadoff man Felipe Alou hit the first and the second home runs in the sixth and eighth innings. The home team trailed 3–2 before tying the score with two out in the bottom of the ninth on a pop fly single by Buchek. St. Louis finally won the game in the 12th, 4–3, when Flood was hit on the helmet by a Phil Niekro knuckleball, went to third on catcher Joe Torre's throwing error on a bunt play, and cantered home on a seeing-eye single up the middle by Lou Brock.

Planning for the stadium began eight years earlier when the Civic Center Redevelopment Corporation was given the power of eminent domain. That power was used to demolish the city's small Chinatown, the Grand Theatre (a strip club), and various warehouses and flophouses to make room for the stadium.

Courtesy Missouri Historical Society, St. Louis

JASTER BLANKS DODGERS FIVE TIMES

September 28, 1966

In a performance as inexplicable as it was superb, rookie left-hander Larry Jaster of the St. Louis Cardinals hurled five consecutive shutouts against the Los Angeles Dodgers in 1966. While the Dodgers relied on pitching, not hitting, to win their second consecutive NL pennant in 1966, Jaster's dominance of their lineup was so complete that the champs were able to get only 24 singles and zero extra-base hits against him in 45 innings of work. He walked eight and struck out 31 in the five games. Ironically, Jaster did not get a chance to face LA in one of the Cardinals–Dodgers series of the season because he was sent to the minor leagues for a month.

A September call-up in 1965, the Cardinals youngster pitched one scoreless inning against the Dodgers in his big league debut and then won three straight starts against other opponents. He split his first two starts in 1966 before besting Claude Osteen on April 25 at Dodger Stadium, 2–0. The Dodgers got seven hits against him, including three in the eighth inning, but a double play kept him out of trouble. After lasting just four innings in each of his next two starts, Jaster was sent down to Tulsa on May 11. He was recalled June 22 and pitched out of the bullpen until manager Red Schoendienst gave him another start in Los Angeles on July 3. He won 2–0 again, beating Don Drysdale this time by allowing only three hits. No Dodger got even as far as second base in the game.

Still unable to crack the rotation, he made only one start in the next three weeks before finally getting another call against Drysdale and the first-place Dodgers. Jaster held them hitless through five innings but allowed three singles in the sixth before inducing Dick Stuart to ground into an inning-ending double play. Two more singles in the seventh were likewise neutralized by a twin killing, and Jaster finished with a six-hit, 4–0 win to earn a spot in the starting rotation. On August 19, he faced Osteen at Dodger Stadium again, winning 4–0, this time on a five-hitter. He also walked three, but the home team was zero for seven with men in scoring position.

His final matchup came on September 28 in St. Louis. The Dodgers were trying to nail down the pennant, while the Cards had lost eight in a row to drop to sixth place. But once again Jaster handcuffed the eventual pennant winners, this time on four hits, to win another 2–0 decision. Los Angeles's biggest threat came in the fourth, when they left the bases loaded. After completing the fifth shutout, Jaster confessed, "It's unbelievable. . . . I don't throw any different against the Dodgers, just up and down, in and out, about 90 percent fastballs."

What Jaster did had never happened before in major league history and has not happened again in all the years since. Grover Cleveland Alexander shut out Cincinnati five times in 1916 but not in consecutive starts.

CUBS' BID FOR FIRST PLACE SNUFFED OUT AT THE PLATE

July 25, 1967

In the 1967 preseason, the Cardinals were picked to finish in the bottom half of the league. But the players expected to be contenders, and they were from opening day. In mid-June they took over first place. The resurgent Cubs caught the Cards in early July but fell back. The Redbird confidence was jolted when Bob Gibson's leg was broken just after the All-Star break. The Cubs nipped at the Cardinals' heels again, and by winning a series opener on July 24, they were once more tied for first. Having finished in dead last in 1966, the Cubs were surprise contenders. And with acerbic Chicago manager Leo Durocher stirring the pot, the Cubs–Cards rivalry was stirring anew.

Nearly 45,000 filled the new Busch Memorial Stadium for the second game of the series. Durocher gambled and lost when he started 22-year-old lefty Rob Gardner, who was knocked out after just eight pitches on hits by Lou Brock, Julian Javier, and Orlando Cepeda. The Cardinals eventually scored three runs in the first inning, though they left the bases loaded. El Birdos added a run in the fourth thanks to aggressive baserunning by Lou Brock. Cardinals starter Ray Washburn, recently recovered from a broken thumb, pitched effectively through eight innings, although Chicago scored two runs in the sixth when Cardinals center fielder Bobby Tolan missed a shoestring diving catch that turned a single into a triple.

Chicago trailed 4–2 in the top of the ninth when Ernie Banks opened with a single. Washburn was relieved by Hal Woodeshick, who promptly hit Ted Savage with a pitch, putting the tying run on base. Ron Willis was rushed in to pitch, and he got two quick outs. Pinch hitter Al Spangler was the Cubs' last hope, and he battled to a full count. The runners were off with the next pitch, and Spangler lined a hit to center field. Tolan cut the hit off and threw to second baseman Javier to keep Spangler, the potential winning run, at first base. Banks scored easily from second while Savage, the potential tying run, barrelled around third trying to score. Javier was alert to the danger, though, and gunned a relay throw to the plate. The throw was right on the money, skipping into catcher Tim McCarver's glove in a perfect position to tag the runner. Savage came in head first and got tagged out on the head before he could snake a hand around McCarver, ending the game.

The win touched off a spurt in which the Cardinals won 11 out of 12 and built a comfortable 8 and a half-game lead on the way to an easy pennant and a world championship.

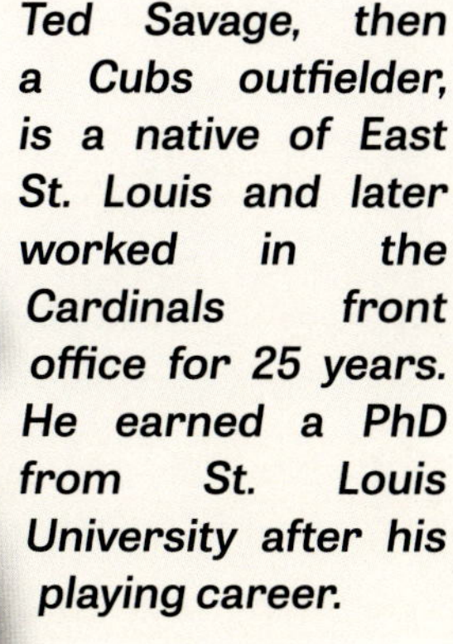

Ted Savage, then a Cubs outfielder, is a native of East St. Louis and later worked in the Cardinals front office for 25 years. He earned a PhD from St. Louis University after his playing career.

Courtesy Getty Images

GIBSON'S THREE WINS BEAT BOSOX FOR CHAMPIONSHIP

October 12, 1967

Displaying an indomitable will to win, Bob Gibson pitched the St. Louis Cardinals to the 1967 world championship by defeating the Boston Red Sox three times for a seven-game World Series triumph.

In 1967, the Cardinals enjoyed a healthy lead in the National League pennant race over the final ten weeks, allowing manager Red Schoendienst and pitching coach Billy Muffet to rest their five-man pitching rotation prior to the World Series. Even though the Redbirds had five different pitchers who logged ten or more wins during the season, Bob Gibson was slated to pitch three games if necessary. Gibby had missed ten starts because of a broken leg and had finished 13–7.

Game 1 in Boston was a neatly executed 2–1 Cardinals victory. The only Boston run came on a home run by the pitcher, Jose Santiago, while Gibson handled every other threat with relative ease. Cards leadoff man Lou Brock scored both runs with the help of Curt Flood and Roger Maris batting behind him. In Game 4 in St. Louis, the Cardinals jumped out to a 4–0 lead in the first inning, and Gibson posted a 6–0, five-hit shutout, putting the Redbirds up in the series, three games to one.

The Red Sox' dream did not die easily, though, and Boston evened the series by winning the fifth and sixth games, setting up a Game 7 showdown. Gibson would be matched against Red Sox ace Jim Lonborg, who had handcuffed the Cardinals lineup in the second and fifth games. Unexpectedly, it was light-hitting Cardinals shortstop Dal Maxvill who got the first big hit of the game, a 400-foot drive off the high center field fence for a three-base hit. Lonborg was able to retire the next two hitters, but Curt Flood rifled a single to center to put St. Louis on top. A ground-ball single by Roger Maris and a wild pitch gave the Birds a 2–0 lead.

Gibson himself muscled up for a solo home run in the fifth inning, and Brock followed up by scoring on a pop-fly single, two stolen bases, and a sacrifice fly. In the sixth, Julian Javier cinched the verdict with a three-run home run over the left field wall. Gibson marched through the Boston batters, fanning 10 and yielding inconsequential runs in the fifth and eighth innings on the way to a three-hitter and a 7–2 victory, his third complete-game win of the series.

An exuberant celebration in the visitors' clubhouse followed, complete with a phone call from President Lyndon Johnson inviting the team to stop at the White House "for cocktails." Manager Schoendienst respectfully declined, and the team winged home to St. Louis for a victory party at Stan Musial and Biggie's Restaurant.

Gibson missed eight weeks during the regular season with a broken leg. In the World Series, he was almost unhittable. He threw three complete games, struck out 26, and allowed just three runs.

Courtesy Getty Images
GAME 4
NATIONAL LEAGUE · AMERICAN LEAGUE
WORLD'S CHAMPIONSHIP GAMES
1967
BUSCH MEMORIAL STADIUM ST. LOUIS
1967 WORLD'S CHAMPIONSHIP GAMES
BUSCH MEMORIAL STADIUM
DO NOT DETACH THIS COUPON FROM RAIN CHECK
NATIONAL LEAGUE · AMERICAN LEAGUE ADMIT ONE · SUBJECT TO THE CONDITIONS SET FORTH ON BACK HEREOF
St. Louis National Baseball Club, Inc.
PLAYED UNDER THE SUPERVISION OF William D. Eckert Commissioner of Baseball
GAME 4
RETAIN THIS RAIN CHECK
NOT GOOD IF DETACHED
ST. LOUIS CARDINALS, AGENT
ENTER GATE 6
SEC. 172
ROW 13
SEAT 6
FIELD BOX PRICE
Taxes Included
$12

GIBSON UNTOUCHABLE IN 15-GAME WIN STREAK

August 19, 1968

Despite being the reigning World Series hero, Bob Gibson got off to a slow start in 1968, posting a lackluster 3–5 record through May. Beginning June 2, however, he ran off a string of 12 consecutive complete-game victories. After an 11-inning no-decision, he won his next three starts with complete games to run his winning streak to 15 games, a St. Louis record. In that 16-game span, he hurled 10 shutouts and four other games in which he allowed only one run each time, and he averaged more than nine innings per start while allowing a total of just 11 runs (10 earned). He allowed more than one run in only two of the starts.

The first win of Gibson's streak, 6-3 over the Mets on June 2, catapulted the Cardinals into first place, and they stayed on top for the rest of the season. By the time Gibson finally tasted defeat again on August 24, the Redbirds were 12 games ahead of their closest pursuers. It's no wonder that the big right-hander was voted the Most Valuable Player in the National League.

Gibson followed his win over the Mets with five consecutive shutouts, setting up a much-ballyhooed matchup against Don Drysdale at Dodger Stadium on July 1. Drysdale had just set a new all-time record with six straight shutouts, and when Los Angeles scratched a run in the first inning on two two-out singles and a wild pitch, Big D's record was safe. But the Cardinals won easily, 5–1, and although Gibson kiddingly blamed catcher Johnny Edwards for allowing his errant pitch to get away, he was very happy with the victory. Picking up where he left off, he pitched four more shutouts in a row. And those official games did not even count a four-inning scoreless stint against the Giants that was rained out.

In his July 30 start against the Mets, Ed Kranepool doubled home a run against Gibson, marking the first RBI against him in 73 innings. The Cardinals won 7–1. In his next start, August 4, the Cubs scored twice in the fifth inning, posting the first "crooked number" against him after a string of 102 innings in which he had allowed only two single runs while putting an even 100 zeroes on the board! Later in the game, Gibson allowed homers to Billy Williams and Al Spangler and fell behind in the top of the 11th inning before his teammates took him off the hook. He bounced back with three more impressive wins, and through August 19, his record was 18–5 with a 0.997 ERA. Gibson's winning streak was snapped by a 6–4 loss to the Pirates, although only three of the Pittsburgh runs were earned. He finished the season with a 22–9 record,13 shutouts, and a stellar 1.12 earned run average.

Courtesy State Historical Society of Missouri

Gibson's 1.12 ERA was the lowest since Mordecai "Three Finger" Brown's in 1906. No one has matched Gibby since. The question often asked is how did he lose nine games that season while pitching 28 complete games and 13 shutouts.

Courtesy Missouri Historical Society, St. Louis

In the World Series, Gibby struck out 35 in 27 innings and allowed just 18 hits with a 1.67 ERA. But he lost Game 7 partly due to a misjudged fly ball by Curt Flood.

GIBSON FANS 17 IN WORLD SERIES GAME

October 2, 1968

In the opening game of the 1968 World Series, Cardinals superstar Bob Gibson gave the world one of the most dominating big-game performances in baseball history, striking out 17 Detroit Tiger batters while winning a five-hit, 4–0 shutout. The win was Gibby's sixth consecutive complete-game victory in World Series competition dating back to 1964 (he would make it seven in a row a few days later), and it forever marked him as a pitching immortal.

The '68 World Series opened on October 2 with an eagerly anticipated pitching matchup between superstar pitchers with superstar statistics: Cardinals ace Bob Gibson and his breathtaking 1.12 earned run average versus Tiger star Denny McLain and his eye-popping 31–6 record. McLain's 1.96 ERA was nothing to sneeze at, nor was Gibson's 22–9 record.

With a capacity crowd and shirtsleeve weather, both hurlers started out very well. Gibson fanned eight in the first four innings, with another out coming on a man caught stealing. McLain pitched out of trouble in both the second and third rounds. But two walks in the fourth followed by singles off the bats of Mike Shannon and Julian Javier gave the Cardinals three runs.

The 3–0 lead was more than enough for Gibson. Rocking back with his hands before coming forward with a violent delivery to the plate that left him nearly parallel to the mound upon release, he completely handcuffed the hard-hitting Tigers. Seeing him for the first time, they were unable to catch up to his high fastballs and were helpless against his low-and-away sliders. Gibby fanned at least one man in each inning, and every Tiger in the starting lineup struck out at least once. A line-drive home run by Lou Brock in the seventh inning gave St. Louis a 4–0 lead.

Going into the ninth inning, Gibson already had 14 strikeouts. After yielding a single to the leadoff hitter, he got Al Kaline swinging for the third time in the game, tying the existing World Series record for strikeouts in a single game and bringing the Busch Stadium crowd to its feet. When Norm Cash chased a breaking ball for his third K of the day, a huge cheer erupted. Catcher Tim McCarver tried to savor the moment by pointing to the message board while walking the ball back to Gibson. The impatient hurler, totally focused on the task at hand, showed little interest in the record and squawked at his batterymate, "Give me the goddamned ball!" Pouring every ounce into each pitch, he overmatched Horton, completely tying him up with an inside breaking ball for the final strike of one the greatest Cardinals performances ever.

With the victory in the books, Bob Gibson could finally break into a broad grin and accept the adulation of his teammates and the St. Louis fans.

CARLTON STRIKES OUT 19 BUT LOSES

September 15, 1969

On a rainy Monday night in St. Louis in 1969, Cardinals left-hander Steve Carlton became the first pitcher in 85 years to strike out 19 batters in a nine-inning game, and the first since the pitching rubber and the sixty-feet, six-inches pitching distance were adopted in 1893. The long-limbed 24-year-old had his fastball hopping and his curve snapping against the first-place New York Mets on this night. Helped by two rain delays totaling 81 minutes, he threw 152 pitches, including 94 fastballs. Carlton struck out at least one batter in every inning and got all nine New York starters plus one substitute at least once, with 10 of the outs coming on called third strikes. This brilliance notwithstanding, Carlton lost the game 4–3, thanks to two mistakes that resulted in a pair of two-run homers by New York slugger Ron Swoboda. The Busch Memorial Stadium crowd gave Carlton a standing ovation nevertheless.

The first six Mets retired all went down on strikes, though two men reached on hits and one on an error. In the third inning, Carlton used his deceptive pickoff move to catch Bud Harrelson off first, leading to some "what might have been" speculation after the game. The Cardinals lost a man at the plate in the bottom of the third when Lou Brock tried to score from first on a dribbler up the middle by Curt Flood, although Flood subsequently scored on a hit by Vada Pinson.

The lanky lefty struck out three in the fourth, but only after Donn Clendenon walked to open the inning, and Swoboda smacked a fat fastball into the seats in left field for his first home run. The Met lead was erased in the fifth when four two-out singles by the home team put the Cards ahead again, 3–2.

Four more Mets fanned in the next three innings before Tommy Agee led off the eighth with a single. Clendenon was called out on strikes before Swoboda struck again, yanking a hanging slider over the boards for his second homer of the game. When Al Weis was called out on a curve ball to end the visitors' eighth, Carlton had 16 punchouts and a chance at the record. Consciously trying for the milestone, he poured it on in the ninth, fanning relief pitcher Tug McGraw and leadoff man Harrelson on four pitches each. Amos Otis, with three strikeouts already, was the last victim, chasing a 2–2 slider in the dirt. Catcher Tim McCarver had to throw to first to record the putout.

Needing a run to tie, manager Red Schoendienst sent a pinch hitter up for Carlton in the bottom of the ninth. Two Redbirds reached base, but McGraw pitched out of the jam to give the Mets the 4–3 decision.

Carlton won 20 games for the Cardinals in 1971 and clashed with owner Gussie Busch over a new contract. He wanted $65,000. Busch ordered him traded to Philadelphia in what many call the worst trade in Cardinals history. Carlton won four Cy Young Awards and 329 games, finished with 4,136 strikeouts, and was inducted into the Baseball Hall of Fame.

A NO-HITTER FOR GIBSON

August 14, 1971

It was a milestone he thought he might never reach, but on August 14, 1971, in his 13th season as a Cardinal, Bob Gibson pitched a no-hit, no-run game. He accomplished the feat against the formidable Pittsburgh Pirates in their own park, winning 11–0 as part of a four-game Cardinals sweep that moved the Redbirds to within four games of the division-leading Bucs. In the end, St. Louis finished in second place, seven games behind, while Pittsburgh went on to win the World Series.

The visitors wasted little time in taking control of the game. Joe Torre and Ted Simmons opened the scoring with RBI singles in the first inning, and Joe Hague followed with a three-run home run, knocking Pirate starter Bob Johnson out of the box. After the five-run first, the Cards added three-spots in both the fifth and eighth. Torre and Simmons each finished with four hits, while Joe Hague and Gibson himself each drove home three runs. Gibby's ribbies came on a sacrifice fly and a two-run single.

On the mound, Gibson was "throwing fire," according to his catcher Simmons. And he was confidently throwing sliders and curves even when behind in the count. Two .300 hitters, Roberto Clemente and Manny Sanguillen, took the night off against Gibson, who struck out 10 batters, including Willie Stargell three times. Three Pirates walked and another reached safely after striking out on a wild pitch. The hardest-hit ball against him came in the seventh inning when Milt May lifted an opposite-field drive to deep left-center. Jose Cruz, however, raced over from center field to make a running catch on the warning track. In the eighth inning, speedy Dave Cash hit a very high chopper to third, but third sacker Joe Torre leaped high to snatch the ball and had just enough time to gun the throw across to first for the out.

The crowd at Pittsburgh's Three Rivers Stadium was cheering for Gibson by the ninth inning, while back in Busch Stadium thousands of fans attending a football Cardinals exhibition game versus Houston were eagerly listening to the baseball broadcast on transistor radios. Vic Davalillo and Al Oliver grounded out to start the ninth, and then Stargell was called out on an explosive slider. "A no-hitter for Gibson!" Jack Buck screamed over the airways as cheers arose in both ballparks.

After overwhelming a powerful Pittsburgh Pirate lineup, the 35-year-old right-hander conceded, "I didn't think I'd ever throw a no-hitter because I'm a high-ball pitcher and high-ball pitchers don't usually throw no-hitters. . . . After it was over I felt like we'd won the seventh game of the World Series."

Courtesy State Historical Society of Missouri

Gibson won 251 games and pitched 255 complete games but just one no-hitter. The game was not televised and the only movie photographer at the game left early, so no video of the end of the game exists.

Courtesy Missouri Historical Society, St. Louis

TORRE'S STELLAR SEASON

September 7, 1971

Joe Torre had big shoes to fill when he came to the Cardinals in 1969 in exchange for former MVP Orlando Cepeda. But fill them he did, winning an MVP Award of his own in 1971, when he had the greatest hitting season by any Cardinal since Stan Musial, pounding out 230 hits while compiling a .363 average and 137 runs batted in.

Buoyed by Torre's potent bat (he had 22 game-winning RBIs), the 1971 Cardinals won 90 games, their best finish between the pennant-winning seasons of 1968 and 1982. Joe turned 31 during the season, and what little running speed he may have once had was gone after many years of catching, so he had few if any "leg hits" in 1971. Playing his first full season as a third baseman, it seemed that every swing he took produced a line drive. And he was remarkably consistent. He rarely had more than 10 hitless at-bats in a row all season, and he hit over .300 against all 11 opposing National League teams.

Courtesy Don Korte

Torre had 21 three-hit games, four four-hit games, and one five-hit game. The five-hit affair took more than five weeks to complete. On August 1 in Philadelphia, Joe was three for five before getting a fourth hit after a long rain delay in the top of the 12th inning. With three Cardinals' runs in, another rain delay ended the proceedings, since the water-vacuuming Zamboni machine at new Veterans Stadium stopped functioning. The umpires ruled that the score would revert to a 3–3 tie through 11 even innings. The Cardinals protested, however, and the league president ruled in their favor, mandating that the game be restarted in the top of the 12th with St. Louis leading 6–3.

The contest resumed on September 7, during the Cardinals' next trip to Philadelphia. Two Cardinals batters were retired to end the top of the 12th, and then the Phillies scored three runs of their own to tie the game. This gave Torre another chance to swing his hot bat, and Joe singled as part of the Redbirds' game-winning, three-run rally in the top of the 13th. Officially, he finished with five hits for the game. In the regularly scheduled contest, Joe was three for four with two runs batted in as St. Louis won another tense, extra-inning game, 7–5. His final hit came in the 10th inning, and he scored the winning run on a rare triple by Ted Simmons. His three RBIs boosted his league-leading margin over Pittsburgh's Willie Stargell to 123 versus 119, and Torre would pull away in the final weeks to a final RBI margin of 137 to 125. He would also win the MVP balloting over runner-up Stargell, with Torre receiving 21 of the 24 first-place votes.

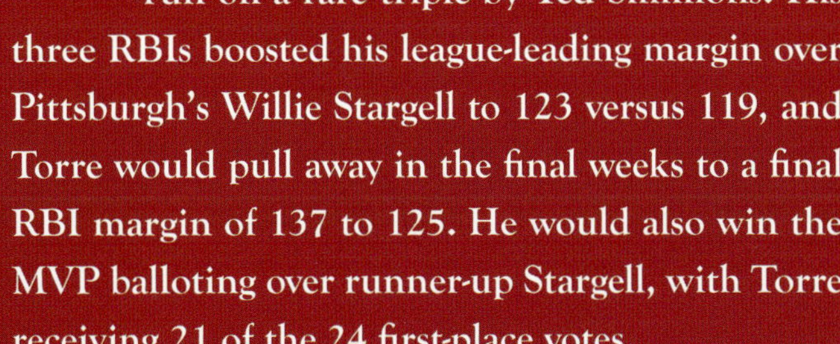

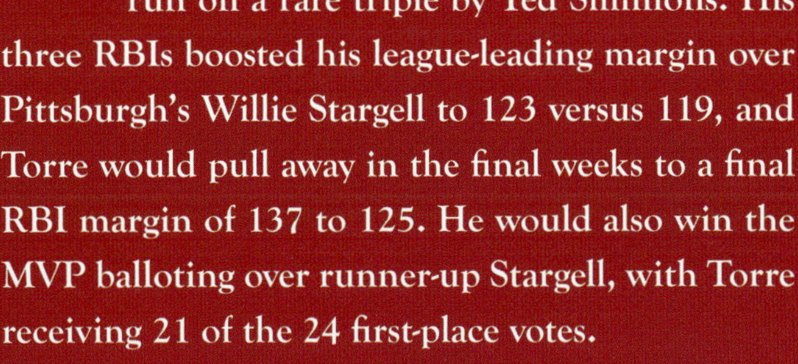

Torre almost didn't make it to St. Louis. The Braves and Mets were close to a deal to send Joe to New York. But the trade fell through, and when the Cardinals offered Orlando Cepeda, the deal was made. Joe had a big challenge because Cepeda was very popular with Cardinals fans.

"MAD HUNGARIAN" STARS ON "WE HLOVE HRABOSKY HBANNER HDAY"

July 12, 1975

When Walter Alston, manager of the defending-champion Dodgers, announced his picks for the National League All-Star Game squad, he chose two established relief pitching stars, Tug McGraw of Philadelphia and Mike Marshall of his own Los Angeles team. Cardinals relief ace Al Hrabosky possessed better 1975 statistics than either of them, including a league-leading 14 saves, as many as Marshall (six) and McGraw (eight) combined.

To honor their star fireman, the Cardinals announced a "Hrabosky Hbanner Hday," slated for the Saturday prior to the All-Star Game. The opposing team was Alston's Dodgers. Hundreds of banners were paraded around the field and some were then put up around the periphery of the park. Many played off the "We Hlove Hrabosky" bumper stickers that had proliferated around town. The theatrical Hrabosky wore a shaggy mane of curly hair and a wide Fu Manchu mustache and was nicknamed "the Mad Hungarian." He was also famous for his occasional "psyching up" interludes, when he would turn his back to the hitter, stalk behind the mound, slam the ball into his glove, and march back to the pitching rubber, finally enraged enough to pitch. He challenged every hitter with his fastball, and his 1.66 ERA for the season showed how effective he could be.

Through most of Saturday's game, the feature was starting pitching, not relievers. Lynn McGlothen, the Cardinals' top hurler, allowed only four hits over eight innings. Unfortunately, one of the hits was a solo home run by Davey Lopes in the fifth inning, giving Los Angeles a 1–0 lead. Al Downing, the Dodger pitcher, did even better than McGlothen. Through the first eight innings, not a single runner reached third against him.

After McGlothen left for a pinch hitter, Hrabosky took over on the mound in the top of the ninth and blew away three hitters. To lead off the bottom of the ninth, Cardinals slugger Reggie Smith picked out a 3–1 fastball and creamed it into the mezzanine seats for a game-tying home run. The blow prompted manager Alston to come out to replace Downing with Marshall, giving the partisan crowd a long chance to boo. The unflappable Marshall retired the next three hitters. Hrabosky matched that by getting three easy outs, including a pinch hitter for Marshall. In the bottom of the 10th against a new pitcher, Rick Rhoden, the Cardinals plated the winning run on a single by Ken Reitz, a sacrifice, and a dribbler up the middle by Bake McBride. That made a 2–1 winner out of the Mad Hungarian.

The exuberant lefty praised the fans and his teammates and even wished Alston and Marshall well in the All-Star Game. As for his own feelings he said, "This was probably the most rewarding feeling I've ever had. . . . This game today was my All-Star Game."

Courtesy Don Korte

Courtesy Getty Images

Al's most memorable game was a nationally televised game on May 9, 1977, against Cincinnati. The game was tied in the ninth inning. He loaded the bases with nobody out. He went into his "Mad Hungarian" routine and struck out George Foster, Johnny Bench, and Bob Bailey, saving the game and sending the crowd into a frenzy.

After breaking Cobb's record, Lou kept running, finishing with 938 steals, one more than the 19th century record set by Billy Hamilton.

Courtesy Don Korte

BROCK BREAKS COBB'S CAREER STOLEN BASE RECORD

August 29, 1977

A rare player who almost seemed to get better with age, Lou Brock's greatest achievements came after turning 30 years old. His 35th birthday came in the midst of his record-setting 118-stolen-base season in 1974. Five of his eight stolen base crowns were won in his thirties, as were seven of his eight batting averages over .300.

One of his most publicized records, breaking the 20th-century career stolen base mark of 892 held by Ty Cobb, was finally achieved with two steals on Monday night, August 29, 1977, in a 4–3 Cardinals loss in distant San Diego. Leading off the first inning, Lou worked Padres starter Dave Freisleben for a walk. With the whole ballpark anticipating a stolen base attempt, Freisleben stared at Brock for a long moment before tossing over to first. Lou, just a few feet from the bag, got back safely. Thinking he now had the edge that he needed, Brock took off on the next pitch. With Brock's great jump, catcher Dave Roberts had no chance, and his throw tailed away from the shortstop and into center field, allowing Brock to pop up from his feet-first slide and advance to third on the error. Lou had tied the record, and the San Diego grounds crew came out and removed the milestone base (second) and presented it to Brock, who was standing on third.

As had happened countless times over his career, Brock's thievery led to a big Cardinals inning, three runs on this night. In the second inning, Lou doubled and moved to third only to be left on base.

The Redbirds held a 3–2 lead when Brock batted in the seventh with a man on first. Lou bounced back to the box, and the runner was forced at second, but the St. Louis speedster could not be doubled up, giving him another opportunity to steal. After a throw to first and a brief time out, Brock was off with the first pitch. Roberts made a strong throw, but it was a little off line, and Lou upended shortstop Bill Almon as he slid in safely with the record-breaking stolen base, number 893.

Like every great base burglar, Lou Brock had an overriding, in-your-face aspect to his game. (Jack Buck called him "the most arrogant player I ever saw.") But he was still widely admired and respected by his opponents. After breaking Cobb's record, players from both teams came out to second base to congratulate him, and Padres player representative Randy Jones told the crowd that Lou "deserved every ovation," and exhorted the crowd, "Let's hear it for Lou Brock." When Lou was removed from the game in the bottom of the seventh, the San Diego fans gave him another tumultuous round of applause.

Courtesy Don Korte

BRUMMER STEALS HOME IN 12TH INNING

August 22, 1982

Courtesy Don Korte

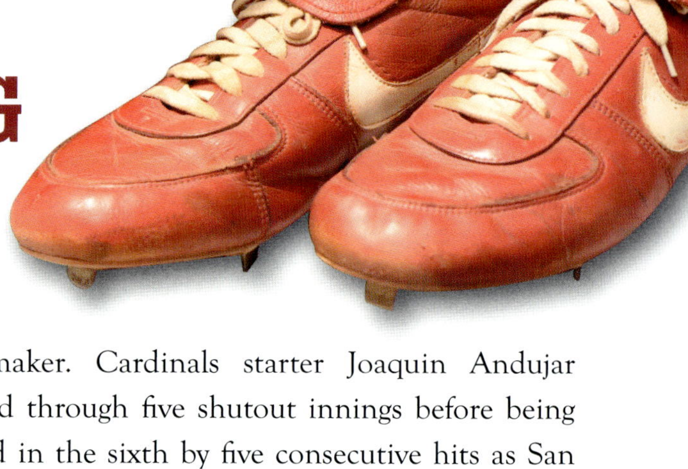

They called it Whiteyball. Under manager Whitey Herzog, the Cardinals hit very few home runs. But they ran the bases with abandon, challenging the opponents to stop them. With solid defense and just enough pitching, that formula brought St. Louis three National League championships in the 1980s.

Perhaps the most unbelievable sample of the Redbirds' daring baserunnning came in the bottom of the 12th inning of a Sunday afternoon game against the San Francisco Giants on August 22, 1982. That was when third-string catcher Glenn Brummer stole home with two outs and two strikes on the hitter to win the game 5–4. Brummer's bold dash took everyone, including his manager, the batter, the pitcher, and even the home plate umpire, by complete surprise. The flabbergasted Giants complained that the pitch was over the plate for strike three, ending the inning and nullifying the run, but umpire Dave Pallone ruled it a ball.

Even prior to the stunning finish, the game had been a tight struggle between two clubs trying to gain ground in their division races. St. Louis got an RBI double by Gene Tenace in the second inning and a two-run home run by Willie McGee in the fourth off Giant starting pitcher Atlee Hammaker. Cardinals starter Joaquin Andujar cruised through five shutout innings before being routed in the sixth by five consecutive hits as San Francisco jumped ahead 4–3. Giant stopper Greg Minton held that lead until two were out in the bottom of the ninth. Ken Oberkfell rescued the Redbirds with a pinch double to left center to send the game into extra innings.

Brummer, who entered the game as a pinch runner in the eighth, singled off Gary Lavelle with one out in the last of the 12th. McGee's fourth hit of the game sent him to second. After a foul out, Ozzie Smith's chopper to the pitcher yielded an infield single, loading the bases. The left-handed Lavelle paid no attention to Brummer leading off third base, and the Cardinals catcher determined that he could swipe home. After a ball and two strikes, he made his break for the plate on the next pitch. Luckily, batter David Green saw him coming and got out of the way rather than swing. Ump Pallone saw him coming, as well, and moved toward the first base side to get a view of the play. Catcher Milt May moved up to get the pitch but could not get the tag down in time to prevent Brummer from sliding home safely.

Although replays suggested that the pitch was a strike and that the umpire was in no position to call it, the "ball" call was official. The Cardinals had the win, and Glenn Brummer had his greatest moment of glory.

Courtesy Missouri Historical Society, St. Louis

It was one of the most unthinkable plays in Cardinals history. Brummer had four steals in 12 career attempts. He told third base coach Chuck Hiller he wanted to steal home. Hiller said no. Brummer did anyway. Giants manager Frank Robinson said home plate umpire Dave Pallone was a liar when he said he called the pitch a ball.

Courtesy Missouri Historical Society, St. Louis

Courtesy Johnmaxmena2
via Wikimedia Commons

AS EASY AS 1-2-3

September 14, 1982

Once Bruce Sutter snagged Mike Schmidt's comebacker, the double play was as easy as one–two–three, Sutter to Porter to Hernandez. Sutter finished John Stuper's shutout, and Darrell Porter's two-run home run beat the Phillies 2–0 and moved the Cardinals back into first place ahead of Philadelphia.

The night before, Monday, Steve Carlton had pitched his Phillies into first place by beating Bob Forsch. Lefty went so far as to hit a home run while skunking his old team, 2–0. On Tuesday, the visiting Cardinals repaid the compliment with a 2–0 shutout of their own. Cardinals rookie Stuper and Phillie veteran Mike Krukow both pitched effectively in tight spots. With men on first and third in the opening inning, Krukow struck out Redbird sluggers George Hendrick and Porter. In the Phillie fourth, Stuper got out of a bases-loaded jam with easy pop outs by Garry Maddox and Manny Trillo.

Having chased a low, slow curve to end the first inning, Porter was determined to wait on the ball when he batted with one on and one out in the fourth. With a count of 1–2, he hung back on a changeup and lined it over the wall in right field to plate the only runs of the game. In the seventh inning, Porter mashed another changeup off the top of the fence, though he was left on base.

The Phillies made their bid to win in the bottom of the eighth. With one out, Stuper walked a pinch hitter and Pete Rose followed with a hard single to center. The Cardinals manager wasted no time bringing in his ace reliever, Sutter. Gary Matthews battled to a full count before hitting a shot toward third. Guarding the line against an extra-base hit, third sacker Ken Oberkfell dived to his left to snare the ball. His first reaction was to try for a double play around the horn, but Rose had been running with the pitch, so Oberkfell double-pumped and threw to first too late to retire Matthews. The bases were loaded.

In stepped reigning NL MVP Mike Schmidt for a classic matchup versus Sutter. The split-finger specialist got two quick strikes before a pair of balls and a couple of fouls. His next 2–2 split-finger fastball was perfectly placed, and Schmidt topped it on a long hop back toward the mound. Sutter had to jump to get it, and the one–two–three double play resulted. Sutter pitched around a one-out walk in the ninth to nail down the 2–0 victory.

The win put St. Louis in first place over Philadelphia, and Herzog's Redbirds never were caught after that. They finished three games ahead of the Phils.

Sutter was an average pitcher coming off shoulder surgery when a minor league coach taught him how to throw the split-finger fastball. He was the first one to use the pitch effectively, and it put him in the Hall of Fame. He's the first major league pitcher in the Hall who never started a game.

"THAT'S A WINNER"—CARDS WIN THE SEVENTH GAME OF THE WORLD SERIES

October 20, 1982

The 1982 World Series pitted teams from two cities with famous beer brewing traditions, the slugging Milwaukee Brewers, nicknamed "Harvey's Wallbangers," versus the St. Louis Cardinals' "Punch and Judy" collection of speed demons. The Brewers had finished first in the majors in home runs, while the Cardinals had finished last, but the series seesawed through six games dead even.

Game 7 was witnessed by a packed house at Busch Stadium and a record television audience. Cardinals shortstop Ozzie Smith electrified the crowd by doing a running back flip before the game got under way.

Each team had its ace hurler primed and ready—Joaquin Andujar for St. Louis and Pete Vuckovich for Milwaukee—and both clipped quickly through the first three innings. In the top of the fourth inning, the Brewers got two hits, but George Hendrick in right field threw Robin Yount out trying to advance to third base to kill the rally. The Cards then scored the game's first run in the bottom half on singles by Willie McGee, Tommy Herr, and Lonnie Smith. The Brewers tied the score on the first pitch of the fifth inning when Ben Oglivie lofted a hanging curveball into the right field seats.

The wheels almost came off for Andujar in the Brewer sixth when he allowed a double, made a wild throw past first on a bunt, and then failed to cover first on a scratch hit as Milwaukee scored twice to lead 3–1.

But the Cardinals bounced right back to regain the lead with three in the bottom of the sixth. With one out, Ozzie Smith slapped a single to right and Lonnie Smith skipped a double into the left field corner. Left-handed reliever Bob McClure came in and walked Gene Tenace to load the bases. Keith Hernandez ripped a 3–1 slider to right center for a two-run single and a tie score. George Hendrick fouled off four pitches before finally slapping an outside serve for a sharp single to right, giving St. Louis the lead, 4-3. In the next inning, Darrell Porter and Steve Braun chipped in RBI singles to run the score to 6–3.

Andujar had blanked the Brewers in the seventh and punctuated the inning by threatening to fight Jim Gantner after the third out. Herzog wisely sent ace reliever Sutter to take over for the volatile starter in the eighth, and Sutter retired all six men he faced. The final out was a long battle with Gorman Thomas, who fouled off four two-strike splitters before finally fanning on a fastball. Cardinals announcer Jack Buck's description of the final pitch—"A swing and a miss! That's a winner, a World Series winner for the Cardinals!"—still holds a revered place in Cardinals lore.

The series matched power against speed and pitching. The Brewers hit 216 home runs during the regular season to just 67 for the Cardinals, who played what has long been called "Whiteyball."

Courtesy Getty Images

FORSCH HURLS SECOND NO-HITTER

September 26, 1983

The 1983 season was bitterly disappointing for the St. Louis Cardinals, as they slipped from the world champions' perch all the way to a sub-.500, fourth-place finish in the NL Eastern Division. Veteran right-hander Bob Forsch, the senior member of the pitching staff, contributed to the decline with a losing season in which he walked too many hitters and served up too many gopher balls. But on the final Monday of the season he salvaged some self-esteem by pitching the second no-hit, no-run game of his career, becoming the first Cardinal to have two no-nos.

Forsch had pitched a no-hitter against the Phillies on April 16, 1978, benefiting from a controversial error ruling in the eighth inning. In this second gem, there were no doubtful rulings.

The defending champs had been mathematically eliminated on Friday night when Steve Carlton posted career win number 300 against them. Only 12,457 paying fans were on hand for the opener of the Expos series on Monday. Forsch came into the game with a string of six consecutive starts in which he had failed to complete six innings, and his ERA of 4.61 was near the bottom of the league list.

But for this one night he had control of all three of his pitches—fastball, slider, and changeup—and he cruised to a 3–0 win. No outstanding defensive plays were required behind him, though Willie McGee's speed in center turned dangerous drives into routine outs in each of the first two innings. The only two runners to reach base against Forsch both got on in the second inning. One was Expos catcher Gary Carter, who had irked the Cardinals with some comments a week before. With two out, Forschie plucked him on the rump, prompting home plate umpire Harry Wendelstedt to warn both teams against further fireworks. The next batter, Chris Speier, smacked a grounder that skittered between second baseman Ken Oberkfell's legs for an obvious error. The misplay put runners at second and third, but Forsch struck out Angel Salazar to end the threat.

The Cardinals got all of their runs against Montreal starter Steve Rogers in the fifth inning. Ozzie Smith, Lonnie Smith, and Willie McGee each drove in a run with a safe hit.

Starting with the Salazar strikeout, Bob retired the last 22 batters he faced, finishing with six strikeouts and no walks while throwing 61 strikes out of 96 total pitches. After the game, clubhouse man Buddy Bates produced a bottle of champagne. It was hardly a pennant celebration, but the bubbly still tasted good as an otherwise sour season for Forsch and the Cardinals was winding down.

Bob is the only pitcher in Cardinals history to throw two no-hitters. His brother Ken also pitched a no-no for Houston. They are the only set of brothers to throw no-hitters in baseball history.

Courtesy Don Korte

CARDS TURN BACK METS IN OCTOBER SHOWDOWN

October 3, 1985

Engaged in a back-and-forth pennant race with the New York Mets all summer, Whitey Herzog's St. Louis Cardinals entered the final week of the season with a three-game lead with six games to play. But the Mets won the first two games of a three-game series at Busch Stadium to cut the lead to one. A win by the despised Mets (dubbed "pond scum" by Cardinals' fans) in the series finale on Thursday would lift them into a tie with the Redbirds.

Tension crackled around the park as a total of more than 50,000 packed the stadium for this final showdown on Thursday, October 3. In the top of the first inning, the Mets got four hits, but somehow Cards starter Danny Cox was able to limit the damage to one run. In the second inning, Terry Pendleton tied the score by racing from first to third on a wild pitch before cantering home on an infield out by Ozzie Smith. Vince Coleman made a clutch catch in left field in the top of the fourth and then lined a two-out, two-run single in the bottom of the inning, putting St. Louis ahead 3–1.

The Mets took a page out of the Whiteyball book in the fifth, when Mookie Wilson went all the way from first to third on a bunt. Wilson scored on a double past first base by Keith Hernandez. In the sixth, however, singles by Smith, Coleman, and Willie McGee put the Birds up by two runs again.

When Cox walked the leadoff hitter in the seventh frame, Herzog went to his "bullpen by committee," first calling in lefty Ken Dayley. He struck out two in a row before Hernandez slapped a double down the third base line. Coleman cut the ball off and held the runner at third base. Herzog next brought in rookie Todd Worrell to face Gary Carter, whose broken-bat pop fly ended the inning. In the Mets' eighth, Strawberry opened with a double and scored on a one-out single by Howard Johnson. Lefty number two in Whitey's pen, Ricky Horton, went in to pitch and got the last two outs in the eighth inning plus the first two outs in the ninth. Hernandez kept the New York hopes alive with a bloop single to deep shortstop, his fifth hit of the game. Herzog brought in Jeff Lahti, his number two right-hander, and on his first pitch, Gary Carter lofted a high easy fly to right fielder Andy Van Slyke for the final out.

The agonizing tension broken, the throng erupted with a long, loud cheer. The hard-won victory put the Cards two games ahead with three to play, and the Birds clinched the division pennant by beating the Cubs on Friday and Saturday.

Hernandez had five hits in that game—maybe a measure of revenge for being traded to the Mets by Whitey Herzog. Hernandez's drug use (cocaine) was the source of friction between the two. His drug use became a matter of public record later at a trial in Pittsburgh.

Courtesy Johnmaxmena2 via Wikimedia Commons

"GO CRAZY, FOLKS!"—OZZIE'S EPIC HOME RUN

October 14, 1985

Courtesy Getty Images

There are a few storied players who have officially finished playoff and World Series games by leaping onto home plate surrounded by a mob of ecstatic teammates. All of those walk-off heroes have been showered by deafening applause from their home crowds. Yet only one of those home run hitters began the contest by going to his fielding position with a hop-skip-cartwheel-backflip, also to the roar of the hometown faithful. That player was "the Wizard of Oz," Ozzie Smith, the sensational Cardinals shortstop. In Game 5 of the National League Championship Series, he drove the St. Louis fans crazy with joy when he hit a most improbable ninth-inning home run to beat the Los Angeles Dodgers 3–2 and give the Redbirds a three-games-to-two series lead.

In Game 5, they jumped on Fernando Valenzuela in the first inning on walks from Willie McGee and Ozzie followed by a two-run double past third base by Tommy Herr. The Cardinals left two men on base in four of the next six innings, but that was all the Cardinals could score against Fernando through eight rounds. In the fourth, the Dodgers tied the count on a two-run homer by Bill Madlock and knocked out starter Bob Forsch. The bullpen by committee of Ken Dayley, Todd Worrell, and Jeff Lahti allowed only two hits and one walk from the fourth inning through the ninth.

With Valenzuela spent after 132 pitches, Dodger manager Tommy Lasorda brought in his ace reliever, Tom Niedenfuer, to pitch the bottom of the ninth. The hulking right-hander retired the leadoff man on a foul pop. Next up was Ozzie Smith. In 1985, the switch-hitter had reached new season highs in hits, RBIs, and batting average. And his six home runs in the regular season doubled his previous best. But all thirteen of his career round-trippers had come while batting right-handed. Batting left, as he did against Niedenfuer, he had no home runs in more than 3,000 at-bats.

Behind in the count 1–2, Ozzie did the unthinkable, golfing a low inside fastball deep to right field. The ball cleared the fence, hit a concrete pillar near the foul line, and bounced back to the outfielder. The umpires signaled home run as Smith pumped his fist, and pandemonium enveloped Busch Stadium. Over the airwaves, Jack Buck screamed with glee, "Go crazy folks, go crazy . . . the Cardinals have just won the game . . . on a home run by the Wizard!" At home plate, Ozzie was smothered by his adoring mates as he jumped onto the plate.

> ***Mention Jack Buck's "Go Crazy" call and most Cardinals fans can tell you what happened. What made Ozzie's home run so incredible is that he had never hit a home run left handed in 3,009 at-bats—until that one off Tom Niedenfuer.***

CARDS RIDE CLARK'S HOMER INTO THE WORLD SERIES

October 16, 1985

Whitey Herzog acquired Jack Clark to be a game changer. Whiteyball had scratched and stolen runs but did not possess a true power threat until 1985, when Jack Clark was installed in the cleanup spot in the lineup with orders to go for the long ball. Vince Coleman had a sensational rookie year in 1985 as the league's best leadoff man. And Willie McGee and Tommy Herr had outstanding seasons in the number-two and number-three spots in the batting order, thanks in part to the presence of the new power threat batting fourth.

Clark's signature moment came in the deciding sixth game of the NLCS at Los Angeles. The Cardinals led the series, three games to two, but Game 6 started out well for the Dodgers. Led by Mariano Duncan (two runs scored and one RBI) and Bill Madlock (an RBI single and a solo home run), the Dodgers built up a 4–1 lead through six innings against Cardinals starting pitcher Joaquin Andujar. St. Louis knocked LA starter Orel Hershiser out of the box in the top of the seventh. Darrell Porter and Tito Landrum opened with clean singles, moved up on a ground out, and scored on a shot up the middle by McGee. Dodger manager Tommy Lasorda brought in his relief ace, Tom Niedenfuer, to face Ozzie Smith. Ozzie, of course, had taken Niedenfuer deep to win Game 5, and this time he lofted a drive toward the short porch in the right field corner. The ball landed on the warning track as McGee scored the tying run and Smith motored to third with a triple. With only one man out, Niedenfuer walked Herr intentionally then blew third strikes past Clark and Andy Van Slyke to preserve the tie. In the eighth, the Dodgers went back ahead, 5–4, on a home run over the right field wall by big Mike Marshall.

With one out in the top of the ninth, McGee singled and Smith walked behind him. Herr's weak ground out to first base advanced the runners to second and third with two gone. The obvious strategy called for walking Clark intentionally, but Lasorda let Niedenfuer pitch to the Redbird slugger. Miffed at this show of disrespect, Clark massacred the first pitch, launching a home run halfway up the left field bleachers to put St. Louis ahead 7–5. The visitors' bench emptied to greet their hero at home plate, and the big celebration began after Ken Dayley retired the Dodgers in order in the bottom of the ninth to close out the game and the series.

On a dramatic home run by their new big bopper, the Cardinals were going to the World Series!

Tommy Lasorda has lived with his decision to pitch to Jack "The Ripper" instead of walking him. He's reminded of it every time he comes to St. Louis. He's tried to justify it by pointing out that Andy Van Slyke was next up. Niedenfuer stuck out Van Slyke in the seventh. There was an audible gasp by the fans in Dodger Stadium when Clark crushed the pitch. Lasorda calls anyone who questions his decision a "second guesser." "A second guesser is someone who can't get the first guess right," says Tommy.

Courtesy Getty Images

It's one of the most famous home runs in Cardinals history. Pendleton hit just twelve out of the park that season. Roger McDowell looked to center field before the pitch. Little did he know Pendleton would crush the pitch over the 410-foot sign.

125 Louisville Slugger

PENDLETON HOMER STUNS SHEA AND SAVES CARDINALS

September 11, 1987

For most of the summer of 1987, the St. Louis Cardinals held a comfortable lead in the NL East race, peaking at 9 and a half games ahead after 93 games played. Slugger Jack Clark was leading the way with 29 home runs and 91 RBIs. But opponents began pitching around "The Ripper" at every opportunity, and the Mets and Expos both started closing in on first place. In a Labor Day series in Montreal, the Cardinals lost three straight, and Clark tore up his ankle in the finale.

The Redbirds limped into New York leading the Mets by one and a half games and the Expos by two. In the series opener, New York jumped on Cardinals ace John Tudor for three runs in the first inning on a run-scoring double by Keith Hernandez and a two-run homer by Darryl Strawberry. St. Louis scratched a run on two walks and two ground outs in the top of the second, but Mookie Wilson's home run in the bottom of the round gave the Mets a 4–1 lead.

New York starter Ron Darling had a no-hitter until Vince Coleman got a bunt single in the sixth, with Darling injuring his thumb on the play. Relievers Randy Myers and Roger McDowell took over for the seventh and eighth innings, respectively, keeping the score 4–1. Ozzie Smith worked McDowell for a walk to lead off the ninth, but an infield out and a K pushed the Cardinals to their final out. With the Met maniacs on their feet anticipating victory, the famous Shea Stadium "Sign Man" flashed placards reading "Only ½ Game Out" and "Only One Hit." McDowell got ahead of Willie McGee, one ball and two strikes, but Willie smacked one under McDowell's glove for a hit to center, scoring Ozzie.

Still down to their last out, the Cardinals now sent Terry Pendleton to the plate representing the tying run. McDowell started him with his patented sinker, which Pendleton fouled off. When Terry stepped back into the batter's box, he surreptitiously snuck in a little farther forward, hoping to use the extra inches to get more lift on the sinker. Attacking the next low delivery, Pendleton golfed the ball over the wall in deepest center field for a game-tying, two-run home run, silencing the stunned crowd.

In the top of the tenth, one-out singles by Coleman and Smith put runners on the corners with one out, and Tommy Herr's line drive single and Dan Driessen's ground out each drove in a run. Ken Dayley closed out the Mets with scoreless innings in the ninth and 10th, giving St. Louis a dramatic, momentum-shifting 6–4 victory. The Mets never got any closer thereafter, and St. Louis won the division title by a three-game margin.

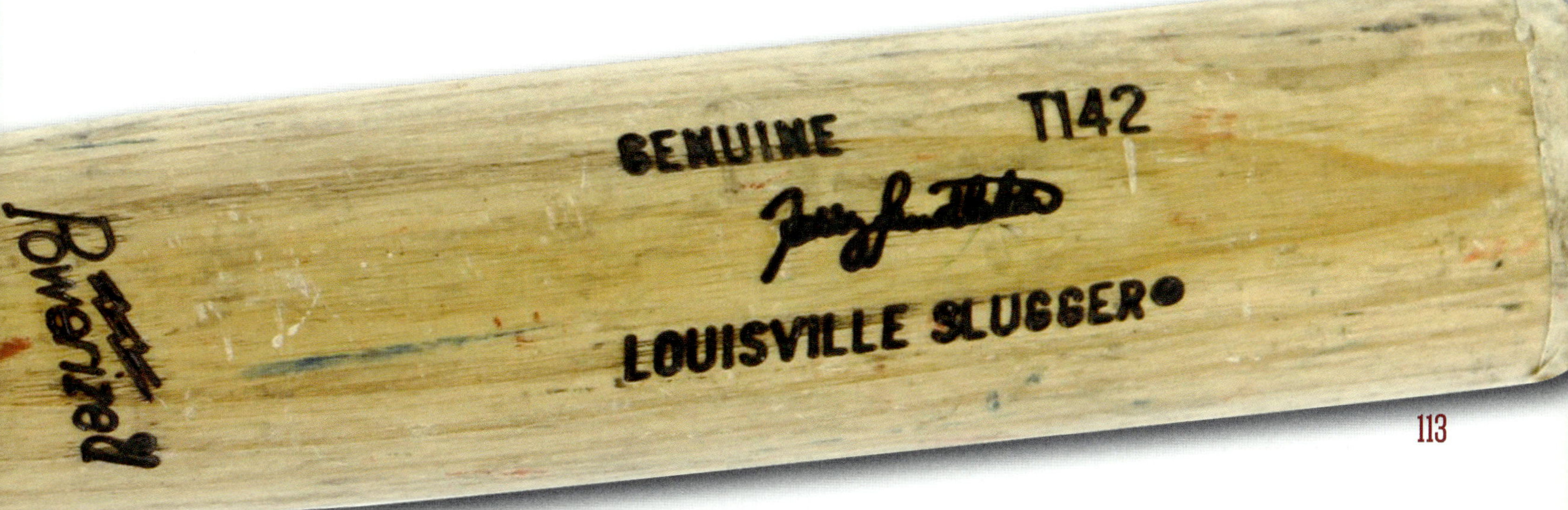

SHUTOUTS VERSUS GIANTS SAVE NLCS

October 14, 1987

When the St. Louis Cardinals and San Francisco Giants squared off in the 1987 National League Championship Series, the Redbirds were without their biggest slugger, Jack Clark, while the Giants came in with big boppers Kevin Mitchell, Jeffrey Leonard, Chili Davis, and Will Clark ready to do damage. Leonard homered in four consecutive games and did it with an insulting "One Flap Down" home-run trot. Davis further riled St. Louis with a disparaging "Cow Town" remark. The Cardinals hung tough but fell behind in San Francisco and came home needing to win Game 6 just to force a Game 7.

The San Francisco starter in Game 6, lefty Dave Dravecky, had completely handcuffed the St. Louis lineup in Game 2, tossing a two-hit shutout. He continued his domination in Game 6 and could hardly be blamed for the lone run put up by St. Louis in the game. Leading off the Cardinals second inning, catcher Tony Peña chipped a broken-bat fly to shallow right field. Lumbering Giant outfielder Candy Maldonado charged in for the catch, only to slide awkwardly at the last instant when he lost the ball in the lights. The ball skipped over him and went to the warning track, allowing Peña to get all the way around to third base. With one out, Jose Oquendo popped a shallow pop fly behind first base. Maldonado galloped in to make the catch, but Peña brazenly tagged up and raced for home. The right fielder's throw arrived in plenty of time but was far up the third base line. Peña evaded the catcher's tag and slapped the plate to score the only run of the game. Fast Cardinals fielding (especially by Willie McGee and Terry Pendleton) and gutty pitching by John Tudor, Ken Dayley, and Todd Worrell blanked the Giants offense for a tense 1–0 win. Southpaw Dayley got the final two outs to seal the verdict with right-hander Worrell patrolling in right field, ready to return to the mound if necessary.

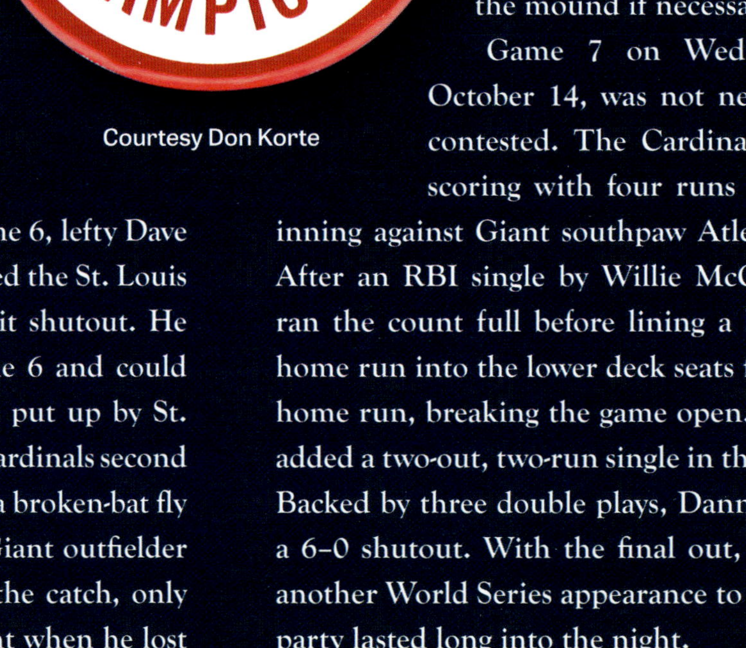

Courtesy Don Korte

Game 7 on Wednesday night, October 14, was not nearly so closely contested. The Cardinals opened the scoring with four runs in the second inning against Giant southpaw Atlee Hammaker. After an RBI single by Willie McGee, Oquendo ran the count full before lining a hanging slider home run into the lower deck seats for a three-run home run, breaking the game open. Tommy Herr added a two-out, two-run single in the sixth inning. Backed by three double plays, Danny Cox pitched a 6–0 shutout. With the final out, St. Louis had another World Series appearance to celebrate. The party lasted long into the night.

The Cardinals pitchers shut out the Giants the last 22 innings of the NLCS. But San Francisco slugger Jeffrey Leonard was named the MVP even though they lost the series. Leonard had 10 hits including four home runs.

Courtesy Getty Images

A WORLD SERIES HOME RUN FOR TOM LAWLESS!?!

October 21, 1987

The 1987 Cardinals played the World Series with severely limited home run power and ultimately lost to the Minnesota Twins in seven games. Terry Pendleton (whose 12 regular-season homers were second on the team) was limited by a rib-cage injury to just seven at-bats, while big bopper Jack Clark (35 homers) was out of action entirely with an injured ankle. The most memorable Cardinals home run of the Fall Classic would come from the unlikeliest source, little-used Tom Lawless.

The lowest of scrubs, Lawless made it onto Whitey Herzog's roster as an emergency everything, the last backup at shortstop, second base, third base, outfield, and even desperation catcher. As such, Herzog held him in reserve through the season, and Tom hit only .080 with just two hits in 25 at-bats in the regular season. After going two for six in the NLCS, Lawless got his most significant playing time (three starts) of the year in the World Series, when he went one for 10.

Down two games to one, St. Louis faced Minnesota's ace left-hander, Frank Viola, in Game 4. Rookie southpaw Greg Mathews, starting for St. Louis, allowed the game's first run when Greg Gagne homered to lead off the top of the third. The Cards tied it in their half on a two-out walk to Ozzie Smith, followed by singles by Tommy Herr and Jim Lindeman.

The Cardinals put the game away with a six-run fourth. Tony Peña led off and was walked on four pitches. Jose Oquendo lined a single over the second baseman. Up stepped Lawless, who had a total of one home run (hit as a Red in 1984) in 384 career at-bats. On Viola's second pitch ("a mediocre fastball," according to Twins manager Tom Kelly) the Cardinals benchwarmer lofted a towering drive deep to left field. The home run cleared the wall by five feet at the most for a home run, while Lawless nonchalantly stayed at home plate admiring the drive. When the ball disappeared, he flipped his bat high into the air and trotted around the bases to a raucous welcome from his teammates at home plate. He later explained that there was no point in running to first base and beyond, since Oquendo was tagging up at first in case the ball was caught. The three-run blast put the Birds ahead 4–1.

St. Louis added three more runs in the inning, one on an RBI single by Lindeman and two on a gapper by Willie McGee. Relievers Bob Forsch and Ken Dayley, backed by some brilliant defense by Ozzie Smith and Vince Coleman, held the Twins to just one more run, as the Cardinals won 7–2 to even the series.

Tom Lawless was the only player ever traded for Pete Rose. Rose was with Montreal and the Reds wanted him back. So, on August 15, 1984, lowly Lawless was sent to the Expos for "Charlie Hustle."

Courtesy Jon Gudorf Photography via Wikimedia Commons

Courtesy Getty Images

FOUR HOMERS AND 12 RBIs FOR WHITEN

September 7, 1993

On the Tuesday after Labor Day, the Cardinals played a makeup game at Cincinnati and suffered a torturous defeat, 14–13. The seesaw contest saw six lead changes as a record 15 pitchers were used. The Cardinals bullpen gave up nine runs in the last four innings, the last two coming in the bottom of the ninth when center fielder Mark Whiten allowed a dipping line drive to get past him for a game-ending triple. Whiten was the only Cardinals position player to go hitless in the slugfest, although he did have a walk, a run scored, and a sacrifice fly.

Luckily for Whiten, there was a doubleheader that night. In the second game, he suddenly got locked into a zone where, in his words, "It didn't matter where the ball was," he was ready to attack it. The switch-hitting outfielder batted from the left side all five times in the game and smashed four home runs to drive home 12 runs, tying long-standing big league records.

Batting sixth in the order, Whiten faced Cincy starter Larry Luebbers in the first inning with the bases loaded and two out. When Luebbers fell behind 2–0, the pitching coach came to the mound for a brief talk while Whiten watched and zoned in. On the next pitch, he golfed a low outside fastball an estimated 408 feet to left center for a grand slam and a four-run Cardinals lead. In the fourth, Luebbers got him to foul out.

In the sixth, Whiten faced Mike Anderson, a rookie making his big league debut, with two men on. Lifting the first pitch of the at-bat 397 feet and over the right-center field fence, Whiten had his second home run while upping his RBI count to seven. Anderson was still around when Whiten came to bat again in the seventh with two on and two outs. He sent a low 2–1 fastball arcing over the fence for another three-run homer, this one estimated at 388 feet.

When the ninth inning came around and Mark batted with one on and one out, it was past midnight in Cincinnati and the Reds were losing 13–2. But the few remaining fans gave Whiten a standing ovation. Fireballer Rob Dibble was the Reds pitcher, and Whiten powdered a 2–0 fastball 448 feet over the center field wall for his fourth home run and 11th and 12th RBIs of the game.

The Cincinnati grounds crew retrieved all of the home run balls and presented them to the beaming slugger after the game. He entered the clubhouse under a ceremonial arch of baseball bats formed by his awestruck teammates. After such a bad first game, it turned out to be quite a night for Mark Whiten.

"Hard-hittin'" Mark Whiten is one of only two major league players to drive in 12 runs in one game. The other player to do it was also a Cardinal. Jim Bottomley accomplished the feat in a game against Brooklyn in 1924. Eighteen players have hit four homers in a game.

Courtesy Getty Images

Courtesy Getty Images

LABOR DAY SERIES SWEEP LIFTS CARDS PAST ASTROS

September 4, 1996

In 1996, his first year as Cardinals manager, Tony La Russa brought pennant race baseball back to St. Louis. In the third year of the new three-division National League, the Cards swapped the Central Division lead with the Astros more than a dozen times during the summer months. The decisive showdown came in St. Louis starting on Labor Day, and the home team swept three in a row from Houston to take over first place for good.

Veterans who had played under laid-back Joe Torre took some time getting used to La Russa. "It was an adjustment," Brian Jordan admitted. "His intensity, his aggressiveness, the way he controls attitudes. But we adjusted. Now everyone wants to play hard."

Ozzie Smith and Willie McGee, two of the older veterans, starred in the Monday series opener on September 2. Ozzie had already publicly announced his impending retirement and privately crabbed about a lack of playing time. Willie, back in Cardinal red after five-plus years in exile, was also given limited duty. After the visitors jumped on St. Louis starter Donovan Osborne for three runs in the top of the first, Ozzie led off the bottom with a double and scored on a single by Willie. In the second, Smith contributed an RBI groundout as the Birds tied the score 3–3. But Houston routed Osborne with a four-run fourth. Undaunted, St. Louis got two runs back on Ozzie's 28th (and final) career home run, off Darryl Kile. The two-out drive hit the top of the right field fence before bouncing over. In the sixth, McGee singled to score Smith again, and in the eighth, Ray Lankford's two-out double plated Luis Alicea to tie the game at 7–7. In the 10th, Ozzie delivered his third hit of the day and was on second when Willie batted with two out. McGee delivered his fourth hit of the day, a chopper up the middle, and Smith slid home just ahead of the throw to score the winning run, ending the 8–7 thriller.

Smith and McGee sat on the bench the next two nights as their teammates completed the sweep. On Tuesday, the Birds slammed out 15 hits in a 12–3 romp, putting St. Louis into first place by half a game. American League imports Todd Stottlemyre (with eight innings pitched) and Gary Gaetti (with a tie-breaking two-run homer) were the biggest stars. In the Wednesday finale, John Mabry and Tom Pagnozzi hit back-to-back homers in the second inning to give Andy Benes a lead he never lost on the way to a 6–4 win.

The Astros left town trailing by one and a half games, and St. Louis won the division by a 7-game margin.

The Cardinals were 62–81 in 1995 and made a dramatic turnaround in '96. The personality of the team changed in the first year of ownership under Bill DeWitt Jr. and the first year in the dugout of Tony La Russa.

Courtesy Don Korte

Totally exhausted, McGwire was given the option of taking the day off. But the stadium was full, and he decided to play against Montreal. In the third inning, he hit home run number 69 off Mike Thurman. In the seventh, he hit magic number 70, a 370-foot blast against rookie Carl Pavano. "I amazed myself," he said afterward. He left St. Louis by the end of the day.

Courtesy Rick Dikeman via Wikimedia Commons

Courtesy Don Korte

70 HOMERS FOR BIG MAC

September 27, 1998

When Mark McGwire signed a contract with St. Louis in September of 1997 he commemorated the occasion with a mammoth home run. He finished that year with 58 homers, and the intoxicating notion grew that this newest Cardinal could break the single-season home run record, Roger Maris's hallowed number of 61. Big Mac stoked the excitement with a grand slam on Opening Day 1998 and an extra-inning walk-off in the next game. By the end of May, he had 27 dingers, far beyond the pace of 10 per month required to challenge the record. Some of muscleman's blasts traveled incredible distances, and media mania and fan infatuation mushroomed. Even his batting practice sessions drew large crowds and broadcast coverage. The Cardinals instituted press-conference style interviews to alleviate the clubhouse crush around his locker.

But there were other sluggers eyeing the prize. Sammy Sosa of the Cubs hit 20 homers in June to close in on McGwire. And Seattle's Ken Griffey Jr. actually caught up to Mac at 37 homers just after the All-Star Break. Sosa finally tied McGwire at 46 homers in early August. Big Mac never slacked off, however, and the Great Home Run Chase gripped the baseball world.

Home runs numbers 61 and 62 came in back-to-back games of a Labor Day series at Busch Stadium against the Cubs, September 7 and 8. Sosa was there of course, and he even received a standing ovation from the St. Louis fans. McGwire's parents and son were in town for the games, as was the Maris family with the bat their father had used for his number 61. The record-tying blow was a typical Big Mac blast that rattled the windows of the Stadium Club against Mike Morgan. The record-setter was a line drive that just snuck over the fence near the left field corner off of Steve Trachsel. McGwire was so hyped up that he missed first base and had to retrace his steps. An impromptu round of hugs followed with the Marises, with his own family, with teammates and even with opponents, especially Sammy Sosa. And St. Louis celebrated the feat long into the night.

The record had been broken, but three weeks of long ball excitement remained. By the next weekend, Sosa had surged into a tie at 62. The final three days of the season began with the friendly rivals tied again at 65. On Friday night in Houston, Sammy went ahead with an early four-bagger, and a dark gloom descended on the crowd in St. Louis. But within an hour, Mac had answered with his own home run. He then hit two more on Saturday and another pair on Sunday. The breathtaking finish hiked his record to an astonishing 70 home runs. Even McGwire said he was "amazed . . . I'm like in awe of myself right now." That awe was shared by baseball fans in St. Louis and around the globe.

Courtesy Don Korte

TATIS HITS TWO GRAND SLAMS IN ONE INNING

April 23, 1999

Records are made to be broken, as everyone knows. On April 23, 1999, Cardinals third baseman Fernando Tatis set a record that will never be broken and quite likely will never be tied: he hit two grand slams in the same inning.

When the Cardinals opened their series in Los Angeles on Friday night, April 23, 1999, the Dodgers used the occasion to honor Mark McGwire for his record-setting home run performance the previous season with special guests and a highlight video for the fans to watch before the game. Southern California fans who were looking for memorable slugging got their wish, but the long-balling came not from the 250-pound Big Mac but from the 170-pound Tatis.

Fernando's big inning came in the third, and there were several turns of events that had to align properly to make his achievement possible. The Cardinals came to bat in the frame trailing the Dodgers 2–0. Darren Bragg led off against right-hander Chan Ho Park with a single, and Edgar Renteria was grazed on the hand by a pitch. McGwire, trying to check his swing, hit a flare to right. Bragg (or third base coach Rene Lachemann) was fooled by the hit and stopped at third, loading the bases for Tatis. Picking out a 2–0 fastball, Fernando ripped a no-doubter deep into the left field bullpen to give St. Louis a 4–2 lead. One out later Eli Marrero homered, and the Cardinals continued to bat around. A couple of throwing errors gave the Cards a sixth run and left the bases loaded for Renteria's second at-bat of the frame. He stroked a single to right, good for another run, but Lachemann held up the runner (pitcher Jose Jimenez) at third. McGwire hit a medium fly ball to right, but Lachemann again surprisingly held Jimenez at third.

So Tatis came up with the bases loaded for a second time in the inning. Incredibly, Dodger manager Davey Johnson left Park in to face him again. Heeding his own manager's advice "to just be patient," Tatis watched the count go to 3–1 before lining a slider into the pavilion seats in left center for another slam. Unbelievable! Fernando thought, "I'm going to fly." No other big leaguer had ever hit two in one inning. Eight RBIs in one inning broke the record of seven set back in 1890 by St. Louis Brown Ed Cartwright. St. Louis went on to win by a 12–5 score, and although he struck out in his last two at-bats on the night, Fernando Tatis had had a game—make that an inning—for the ages.

> ***Baseball history is full of random, mind-boggling, insane events, none more insane than April 23, 1999. Twelve players have hit two grand slams in one game. But no one had hit two slams in the same inning until Tatis did it. And he hit them off the same pitcher—Chan Ho Park. Why was he still in the game?***

Courtesy Don Korte

Courtesy Getty Images

EDMONDS'S HOMER GIVES CARDS THIRD STRAIGHT WALK-OFF WIN VS. METS

September 3, 2000

For the second time in three days, Jim Edmonds came hopping into the arms of his teammates at home plate following a walk-off home run. On the day in between, Fernando Viña had been mobbed by the Redbirds for delivering a game-ending RBI single. All three sudden-death victories came over the New York Mets, a team that had been 6–0 versus St. Louis before the series. The sweep kept the Cardinals nine games ahead of the second-place Reds in the NL Central, while the Mets slipped half a game behind the Braves in the NL East. It also gave St. Louis a much-needed confidence boost against a team they could very well meet in the playoffs.

The Friday night series opener was a seesaw affair, with the Cards owning leads of 1–0 and 4–3, while the Mets overtook them twice for leads of 3–1 and 5–4. Edmonds tied the game 5–5 with a two-out RBI single in the seventh inning and then won it in the bottom of the ninth with a one-out home run off Pat Mahomes. A victory dance at home plate ensued, with Jimmy E and his mates hopping up and down in unison. Mike Matheny earned honorable mention by getting two hits and throwing out three runners attempting to steal.

On Saturday the Cardinals' Darryl Kile hooked up with former teammate Mike Hampton of the Mets in a tight pitching battle. Kile went the distance, but with the score 1–1 and a runner on second and one out in the last half of the ninth inning, Hampton was removed for closer Armando Benitez. After a walk and a strikeout, Viña came through with the two-out walk-off hit to right, setting off another celebration.

In the Sunday finale, rookie Rick Ankiel allowed the Mets only two hits in seven innings but left trailing 1–0. New York starter Glendon Rusch pitched seven shutout frames, but in the eighth, St. Louis pinch hitter Placido Polanco knocked a pitch from reliever Dennis Cook over the left field wall for a three-run home run, his first homer since April. Cardinals closer Dave Veres, however, served up a two-run homer to Bubba Trammell in the ninth, and the game went into extra innings.

Leading off the bottom of the 11th against burly Rick White, Edmonds picked out a fastball away (and "up a little bit") and lofted it into the right field seats, 392 feet away, to win the game 4–3. He and his team then gave a repeat performance of the home plate victory hop and followed it up with a raucous celebration in the clubhouse. "The boys are into it," manager Tony La Russa marveled. It had, indeed, been a marvelous weekend.

> ***Bitter losing pitcher Rick White said, "For Edmonds to hit both of them is even worse. He's more of an 'I'm the hero guy' instead of just 'we won.'" Edmonds said it was "unfortunate that a guy who doesn't have any idea who I am would say something that silly."***

Courtesy shgmom56 via Wikimedia Commons

Courtesy majorvols via Wikimedia Commons

FLAGS AND PATRIOTIC POETRY MARK CARDINALS' RETURN TO PLAY

September 17, 2001

Six days after the suicide plane hijackings and crashes in New York, Washington, and Pennsylvania, Major League Baseball returned to regular season play in six cities, including St. Louis. At Busch Stadium, the occasion was marked by a poignant remembrance of the victims, a heartfelt tribute to the police and firefighters here and everywhere, and a patriotic poem by legendary Cardinals broadcaster Jack Buck. Flags were everywhere, from small ones given out at the gates to larger ones unfurled in the stands to the gigantic one spread over the field for "The Star-Spangled Banner." The loudspeakers blared not just with the national anthem but also with Lee Greenwood's "God Bless the USA," which the crowd sang with fervor. Then the Cardinals went out and won the game 2–1, to move into a tie for the wild-card lead in the National League.

For the Cardinals players as well as the visiting Milwaukee Brewers, it was good to get back to work, but it was anything but a normal night at the park. "It's hard for me to describe," said Brewer right fielder Jeremy Burnitz. "There was a big sense of patriotism. . . . As a player, it was not business as usual." During the pregame presentations, Cardinals catcher Mike Matheny admitted, "Everybody is fighting back tears and by the end you hear people chanting U-S-A! . . . Our emotions and hearts were beating fast."

When the actual game got under way, the starting pitchers were sharp, although some of the other players showed signs of rust. Bulky Milwaukee right-hander Ruben Quevado and skinny St. Louis lefty Bud Smith both looked dominant through the first four innings. But Brewer third baseman Lou Collier fumbled the first ground ball hit his way. And Cardinals rookie Albert Pujols got doubled off after straying too far off first base as Burnitz made a leaping catch at the wall.

In the Milwaukee fifth, right fielder J. D. Drew failed to glove Devon White's long drive to right field for a two-base error, and White came around on two groundouts to score the game's first run. Drew atoned for his error by throwing a runner out at the plate to end the inning. St. Louis staged the winning rally in the sixth with one-out doubles by Placido Polanco and Drew and an RBI single by Pujols.

Smith, who was making his first start since pitching a no-hitter in San Diego on September 3, got through seven innings while allowing only three hits, one base on balls, and one unearned run. Reliever Gene Stechschulte loaded the bases in the eighth, but lefty Steve Kline got out of that jam and made quick work of the ninth inning for the save. The demonstrative Kline later confessed that, "Before the last out, I started to shake. I was trembling. It was such an overwhelming experience."

Jack Buck loved to write poetry, and he brought his "9-11" poem into the KMOX sports office. It gave the staff chills. It was put to music and played on the air. Cardinals management invited Jack, who was suffering from Parkinson's disease, to read it on national TV when the season resumed. It was one of his last public appearances.

Courtesy Getty Images

INSPIRATION FROM KANNON KILE IN PLAYOFF WIN

October 12, 2002

No St. Louis sports club suffered more heartbreak than the 2002 Cardinals. All of Cardinals Nation was saddened by the passing of Jack Buck at age 77 after a long illness on June 18. Then the players were devastated by the sudden death of Darryl Kile in his hotel bed in Chicago on June 22. The pitcher was just 33 years old and apparently perfectly healthy when a congenital heart defect suddenly killed him in his sleep. The shocked ball club went back to work the next day, but only after Kile's widow, Flynn, said "she wanted us to win a World Series ring for Darryl."

And no St. Louis sports club ever performed more valiantly than the 2002 Cardinals. It took a while to get past the grief (Matt Morris lost nearly 20 pounds at one point), and the team played only .500 ball for the next six weeks. With Kile's number 57 jersey in their dugout, they roared through the final seven weeks of the regular season at a 37–12 clip. When they raced through the first round of the playoffs, sweeping the defending world champion Diamondbacks, a series ring for Darryl looked possible.

The storybook scenario, however, faltered quickly in the NLCS when the wild-card Giants won the first two games of the series. Desperately needing a victory in Game 3, the Cardinals got inspiration from five-year-old Kannon Kile, who visited the team with his mother for the first time since his dad's tragic death. Dressed in a number 57 Cardinals uniform, the boy lined up with the team for pregame introductions and was given a warm ovation by the fans in San Francisco. For the St. Louis players, "It was an inspiration having him there," and during the game he did a few turns as batboy.

Kannon was five years old when Darryl died. He, like his father, grew up to 6′5″ and is a star athlete. But his sport is not baseball, something he found boring. He has excelled in volleyball. He says he doesn't remember too much about that day at Busch Stadium when he threw out the ceremonial first pitch.

And the Cardinals got a hard-fought, 5–4 win. Veteran Chuck Finley, a midseason acquisition to fill Kile's spot in the rotation, got his first career postseason win in what would be the last game he played before retiring. He pitched around some shaky early defense and got the Giants to leave the bases loaded in the first two innings. Finley even scored a run himself after striking out on a wild pitch, and Jim Edmonds and Mike Matheny each homered to build a 4–1 Cardinals lead. In the Giant fifth, however, Barry Bonds blasted a long three-run home run to tie the score.

Courtesy Don Korte

Eli Marrero got the lead right back with a solo homer leading off the Cardinals sixth. From there, Dave Veres, Steve Kline, Rick White, and Jason Isringhausen patched together four scoreless innings of relief pitching to nail down a 5–4 win. After the game, an impish Kannon Kile slid over home plate, and then his Cardinals "teammates" carried him off the field. For one day at least, they could think of Darryl Kile and have something to smile about.

EDMONDS'S 12TH-INNING HOMER WINS GAME 6

October 20, 2004

The 2004 Cardinals had come into the National League Championship Series as a team confident in its talent and optimistic about its destiny. The Birds had won 105 games in the regular season and had brushed aside the Dodgers in the first round of the playoffs. They started the second round at home and won the first two NLCS games 10–7 and 6–4.

Their NLCS opponents, the Houston Astros, had entered the series just as confidently. They sported the famous "Killer Bees" lineup, which featured Craig Biggio, Carlos Beltran, Jeff Bagwell, and Lance Berkman in the first four slots in the batting order. Backing up the Bs was Jeff Kent, who hit two game-winning home runs as the Astros won the next three games of the series, all played in Houston.

So the Cardinals came home for Game 6 on the brink of elimination. St. Louis built a 4–3 lead on a two-run homer by Albert Pujols in the first and a two-run single by Edgar Renteria in the third. The home field also helped, since the hot-hitting Beltran whacked two drives off the right field wall on the fly during the game. Each blast would have been a home run in Houston, but in St. Louis right fielder Larry Walker played both balls perfectly and held Beltran to a single each time. After Jason Isringhausen pitched a one-two-three eighth, he went back out to close the game in the ninth. But a two-out RBI single by Bagwell tied the score.

When "Lights Out" Brad Lidge came in to pitch for Houston, the Cardinals seemed doomed. Lidge limited St. Louis batters to an anemic two for 55 (.036) in 2004, capped by a nine-up-nine-down stint in this game. But the Birds hung in. Izzy added a scoreless 10th inning, and Julian Tavarez put up zeroes in the 11th and 12th. The high-strung Tavarez had suffered a self-inflicted finger injury after giving up the decisive homer to Beltran in Game 4 in Houston, but in Game 6 he pitched aggressively and effectively despite a heavily bandaged left hand.

In the bottom of the 12th, the Astros removed Lidge and brought Dan Miceli in to pitch, and a wave of optimism swept the park. With one on and one out, Jim Edmonds let fly with his uppercut swing and sent a high fastball soaring over the bullpen to win the game 6–4. The long day of built-up tension exploded into jubilation as Jimmy E gave a triumphant double-fisted salute and sailed around the bases to an energized greeting at home plate.

There was, of course, another game to win, and there would be more Cardinals heroics. But the exhilaration of the moment had seldom been matched at the old ballpark.

Houston twenty-game winner Roy Oswalt was ready in the bullpen, but Astros manager Phil Garner decided on six-game winner Dan Miceli to pitch in the 12th. Fatal mistake. Edmonds, who hit 42 out of the park in the regular season, hit a moon shot for the game winner.

Courtesy Getty Images

"MV3" LEAD BIRDS PAST CLEMENS AND 'STROS IN GAME 7

October 21, 2004

The biggest heroes of the season provided the biggest heroics of the night as St. Louis came back to beat Houston, 5–2, to win the decisive Game 7 of the 2004 National League Championship Series. The triumvirate of Albert Pujols, Scott Rolen, and Jim Edmonds starred as the Cardinals beat Astros ace Roger Clemens to take the decisive game in what was one of the most hard-fought and exhausting series in club history. Other Redbirds came up big as well, of course, especially winning pitcher Jeff Suppan and pinch hitters Roger Cedeño and Marlon Anderson.

After the tense, 12-inning drama of Game 6 the previous evening, the Game 7 crowd at Busch on Thursday, October 21, was primed to celebrate. But the Astros were not about to roll over and play dead. Indeed, Craig Biggio led off the game with a home run to put Houston ahead from the very start. In the second inning, they made a bid to break the game open after putting two men on with one out. Brad Ausmus cracked a drive up the gap in left center that seemed destined to score both runners. But Gold Glover Edmonds got a great jump, raced across the outfield, and made a full-out dive on the grass to snatch the ball for a miraculous catch, squelching the rally. Cardinals killer Carlos Beltran did score another run for Houston in the third on a walk, stolen base, fly out, and error, putting the home team behind 2–0.

Starting pitcher Suppan settled down after that and aided the offense with a deft squeeze bunt to bring home Tony Womack in the bottom of the third, cutting the deficit to 2–1. Suppan was removed in the bottom of the sixth for Cedeño, who delivered a pinch single and moved up on two infield outs. Facing Clemens with two strikes and two outs, Pujols stayed on an inside pitch and doubled near the left-field line, driving Cedeño home. Rolen then ambushed the Rocket's next delivery, another one in on the fists, and lined it deep into the corner. The ball barely cleared the fence just a few feet fair for a two-run homer, giving the Cards the lead and sending the city into euphorics.

Anderson doubled in the eighth and scored an insurance run on a hit by Larry Walker. Kiko Calero, Julian Tavarez, and Jason Isringhausen combined for three hitless innings of relief pitching to nail down the victory and earn the Cardinals a berth in the World Series for the first time in 17 years.

Edmonds said, "I knew if I didn't catch that ball, we were going to lose that game. The ball's hit. You're like, 'Uh oh, I've got to catch this.'" Astros manager Phil Garner said, "We're stunned. There's no way he catches the ball. Absolutely no way." It was one of the best catches in Cardinals history.

Courtesy Don Korte

Courtesy Getty Images

Courtesy Djh57
via Wikimedia Commons

Want to win a trivia bet? Chris Duncan hit the Cardinals' last regular-season home run at Busch Memorial Stadium. Albert Pujols hit the Cards' last home run ever there in Game 2 of the NLCS. But the last home run hit at Busch was by the Astros' Jason Lane in Game 6. Lane had hit a career-high 26 homers in the regular season.

PUJOLS MOON SHOT IN HOUSTON MEANS ONE MORE GAME FOR "OLD BUSCH"

October 17, 2005

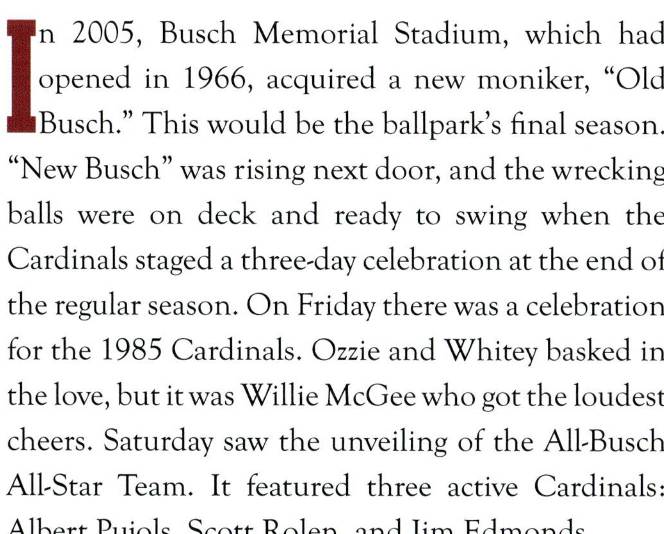

In 2005, Busch Memorial Stadium, which had opened in 1966, acquired a new moniker, "Old Busch." This would be the ballpark's final season. "New Busch" was rising next door, and the wrecking balls were on deck and ready to swing when the Cardinals staged a three-day celebration at the end of the regular season. On Friday there was a celebration for the 1985 Cardinals. Ozzie and Whitey basked in the love, but it was Willie McGee who got the loudest cheers. Saturday saw the unveiling of the All-Busch All-Star Team. It featured three active Cardinals: Albert Pujols, Scott Rolen, and Jim Edmonds.

For the Sunday finale, adoring throngs arrived early and stayed very late, misty-eyed with their emotions. "They will be tearing down a part of my life," sobbed Sara Dayley, daughter of '85 reliever Ken. Mike Shannon and Red Schoendienst did first-pitch duty, given that they had seen more games here than anyone else. After the game, the Budweiser Clydesdales galloped around the park for the first time in 10 years. More than 100 old Cardinal players in Birds-on-the-Bat jerseys were introduced to the throng, and the field became a swirl of hugs, handshakes, and tales of old.

The Cardinals swept the series that weekend to finish the regular season with 100 wins. Rookie Chris Duncan hit the last home run. It was his first in the big leagues, bringing a smile to the face of his usually taciturn father, Dave, the longtime Cardinal pitching coach.

But there would be more baseball at this Busch Stadium in the NL playoffs. A Reggie Sanders grand slam was the highlight in a first round three-game sweep of the Padres. And the Cards beat the Astros in Game 1 of the League Championship Series. But Houston won the next three games and held a 4–2 lead with two out in the ninth inning of Game Five. "Lights Out" Brad Lidge was his usual dominant self against St. Louis, putting the Astros one out away from their first World Series. With Minute Maid Park in Houston roaring in anticipation, David Eckstein was able to prolong the Cardinal season with a hit through the left side. And Jim Edmonds walked to put the tying runs on base.

Up strode the mighty Albert Pujols. After taking the first pitch, he launched the next one nearly into orbit. Astros fans gasped and fell silent as the ball rattled the upper reaches of the left field structure for a monstrous home run. Suddenly trailing 5–4, the Astros went out quickly in the bottom of the ninth. There would be another game back in Old Busch Stadium, after all.

Sadly, St. Louis lost Game 6 at home, 5–1, ending the saga of the old ballpark.

CARDINALS OPEN NEW BUSCH STADIUM

April 10, 2006

Part of the left field grandstand was not finished, newspapermen were grieved by the inadequate view of the field from the pressbox, a visiting Milwaukee Brewer hit the first home run, and baseball commissioner Bud Selig had to address questions about steroid use. But all in all, the official opening of the Cardinals' new Busch Stadium in 2006 was a swimming success. The weather was perfect, the vista including the Arch and the Old Courthouse was stunning, and the home team won 6–4 on the strength of Mark Mulder's pitching and hitting.

Built on a plot overlapping the old Busch Memorial Stadium, the upper decks in left field were not ready by opening day, holding down the attendance to 41,936 paid (capacity was due to increase to 46,831 by midseason), but many more enthusiasts came just to be near the action, spending the game outside the gates. They got to witness the rededication of the relocated Musial statue and cheer The Man. For those inside, there were the usual festivities: Clydesdales and Hall of Famers paraded around the warning track before the current players made the same circuit.

For the record, the first official pitch was a ball from Mulder to Brewer leadoff man Brady Clark, who lined out to second baseman Aaron Miles on the next pitch. Brewer cleanup man Carlos Lee got the first hit, a line single to center leading off the second inning. Bill Hall homered into the first row of the bleachers in right center on Mulder's next pitch, scoring the first two runs. Albert Pujols led off the bottom of the third with the first Cardinals home run, a 445-foot liner high into the seating in

Courtesy Don Korte

Courtesy Getty Images

left center against Milwaukee right-hander Tomo Ohka. Later in the inning, Jim Edmonds scored the tying run on a sacrifice fly by Yadier Molina.

Mulder started a two-run rally in the bottom half of the fourth with a leadoff walk. Scott Rolen came through with a bases-loaded double down the left field line with two out. Batting against reliever Rick Helling, Mulder doubled over the center fielder's head in the fifth for the first extra-base hit of his big league career. Against Jose Capellan in the seventh, he went himself two better, capping a nine-pitch at-bat with a two-out, two-run homer over the wall in right center, upping his lead to 6–2 and earning the stadium's first standing ovation. Mulder got another standing O when he left the game in the top of the ninth. Although the Brewers scored twice in the frame and left the tying runs on base, Jason Isringhausen was able to finally close out the game.

Baseball heaven or not, the new Busch Stadium's inaugural performance was wonderful for Cardinals fans.

There have been a number of ballparks where professional teams have played in St. Louis. Robison Field (1892–1920), Grand Avenue Grounds (later Sportsman's Park and Busch Stadium) (1875–1966), Busch Memorial Stadium (1996–2005), and Busch Stadium (2006–present). Negro League teams played at a variety of ball fields. Stars Park was the most famous (1922–1931).

Courtesy All-Pro Reels via Wikimedia Commons

MOLINA'S NINTH-INNING HOMER BEATS THE METS IN GAME 7

October 19, 2006

With a spine-tingling ninth inning that featured a two-run home run and a game-ending called third strike with the bases loaded, the St. Louis Cardinals won the franchise's 17th National League championship by taking Game 7 of the 2006 NLCS in New York, 3–1.

The decisive game was a tense pitchers' duel between the Cardinals' Jeff Suppan (12–7 for the regular season) and the Mets' Oliver Perez (3–13). New York took a 1–0 lead in the first inning on a hustle double by Carlos Beltran and a broken bat flare by David Wright that fell in safely behind first base. The Cards answered with a run in the second on hits by Jim Edmonds and Molina and a deftly pushed safety squeeze bunt by Ronnie Belliard.

Although the score remained 1–1 until the ninth, the sixth inning witnessed one of the plays of the century. With one on and one out, Scott Rolen drove a pitch on a high line toward the bullpen in left. Outfielder Endy Chavez raced back and, with no time to set himself, made a twisting leap at the warning track. Reaching high and far beyond the fence, Chavez snared the ball in the webbing of his glove and snatched the snow cone back into play, robbing Rolen of a two-run homer and doubling the man off first base for good measure.

Shea Stadium broke into a frenzy, which was heightened when a two-base throwing error in the bottom of the sixth put Mets on second and third with one out. Suppan, however, was equal to the emergency, fanning Jose Valentin before retiring Chavez on a routine fly ball.

Both starting pitchers were gone by the ninth inning. Against Met righty Aaron Heilman, Rolen fouled off four two-strike pitches before smacking a one-out single past the shortstop. Molina, a .216 hitter with only six four-baggers in the regular season, then jumped all over a hanging changeup, sending it so far over the bullpen wall that Chavez had no chance for another miracle.

Young Adam Wainwright, who had taken over the closer's role for St. Louis in September, gave up singles to Valentin and Chavez to start the bottom of the ninth. Pinch hitter Cliff Floyd took a called third strike on a curveball for the first out. Jose Reyes lined out to center before Paul LoDuca walked on five pitches, loading the bases. The batter was Beltran, a man with seven homers and a .360 average in 14 NLCS games versus St. Louis. After taking a strike-one fastball, Beltran fouled off a curve. Wainwright then snapped another curve over the heart of the plate, leaving Beltran frozen for a called strike three. Game over. Series over. Despite posting just 83 regular-season wins, the overachieving Cardinals were going to the 2006 World Series.

Cards rookie closer Adam Wainwright loaded the bases in the bottom of the ninth. Two out and Carlos Beltran at the plate. He'd hit 41 homers during the regular season and three more in the NLCS. Two strikes. Wainwright said to himself, "I'm going to throw the best curveball that I can possibly throw." He did. "I threw the best curveball I've ever thrown." Strike three. Game over.

CARDS BEAT TIGERS IN FIVE FOR WORLD CHAMPIONSHIP

October 27, 2006

Completing an improbable October run, the 2006 St. Louis Cardinals ended the franchise's longest world championship drought at 24 years when they defeated the Detroit Tigers in five games. For manager Tony La Russa, the title was finally won in his 11th year at the Cardinals helm.

In clinching Game 5, Cardinals' starting pitcher Jeff Weaver, a midseason acquisition, outpitched Tiger rookie Justin Verlander and, aided by key errors, got the 4–2 win. Verlander was very wild in the first inning, hurling two wild pitches while walking the bases loaded. But shortstop Carlos Guillen saved two runs with a fine pickup and acrobatic throw to end the threat. With a man on third and two out in the Cardinals second inning, David Eckstein hit a shot down the third base line. Brandon Inge made a diving stop only to throw wildly past first, allowing Yadier Molina to score the game's first run.

In the top of the fourth, a Cardinals error opened the way to a pair of Tiger runs. With one out, right fielder Chris Duncan muffed an easy fly ball for a two-base miscue. Sean Casey, batting next, turned on a Weaver fastball and lined it into the seats inside the right field foul pole for a two-run homer, giving Detroit a brief 2–1 lead. St. Louis bounced right back with two runs in the bottom of the inning. Molina singled with one out and moved to second when So Taguchi scooted a hit up the middle. Pitcher Weaver came up in a sacrifice situation, but his bunt was too hard. Verlander pounced on it and tried for the force at third base. But his throw was way wide, and Molina scored the tying run as Taguchi and Weaver wound up at second and third. It was the fifth straight game in which a Tiger pitcher had made an error. Shellshocked, Detroit manager Jim Leyland decided to keep his infield back, and Eckstein's groundout to short drove Taguchi home with the go-ahead run.

Weaver got settled into an effective pattern and allowed only two baserunners in the next four innings. His teammates gave him an insurance run in the seventh. David Eckstein's grounder to short turned into a hit when Guillen laid back on a high hop and threw too late to first. Eck scored on a two-out single by Scott Rolen.

Young Adam Wainwright came in to close the game in the ninth inning. He gave up a one-out double and a two-out walk before striking out Inge to end the game. As an emotional (for him) La Russa put it, "When you're around here you can't 'join the club' until you win a World Series." Now Tony had finally joined the ranks of Cardinals world champions.

Improbable. Detroit was 95-67 in winning the American League pennant. The Cardinals struggled through their first season in the new Busch Stadium, finishing just five games over .500 (83-78). That's the second worst record ever for a team reaching the World Series. (The worst? The 1973 New York Mets.)

Courtesy Missouri Historical Society, St. Louis

Courtesy Getty Images

Courtesy Johnmaxmena2 via Wikimedia Commons

HOLLIDAY'S RED-HOT REDBIRD START

August 1, 2009

Matt Holliday made his major league debut in St. Louis on April 16, 2004, as the starting left fielder for the Colorado Rockies and promptly missed the first fly ball hit his way. But he quickly established himself as a big league star and was a much sought-after player when the Cardinals acquired him in a trade with the Oakland Athletics on July 24, 2009. As a potential free agent likely to draw strong interest from both leagues after the season, his future in St. Louis caused much speculation. General manager John Mozeliak suggested that once we "let him get a taste of St. Louis," a long-term contract agreement could be reached.

In his first game with his new team, the Stillwater, Oklahoma, native got four hits, and he finished the series seven for 11. The torrid hitting continued through a four-game series versus the Dodgers in St. Louis, when Holliday went six for 19 and received a warm welcome from the Busch Stadium faithful.

Next came a weekend series against the Astros. On Friday night, Matt went four for four. His final hit of the game, an eighth-inning double, drove home Albert Pujols with the tying run, and Holliday crossed the plate with the go-ahead run minutes later. The 4–3 victory moved the Cardinals back into first place, half a game ahead of the Cubs.

His meteoric start reached its apex the next night, Saturday, August 1. The game figured to be a pitchers' duel. Each starter, Wandy Rodriguez for Houston and Chris Carpenter for the Cardinals, had gone 4–0 in July. Carpenter had a 1.75 ERA for the month, and Rodriguez had a nifty 0.75 mark. But Rodriguez had to leave the game in the fifth inning after pulling a hamstring trying to beat out a bunt. Carpenter stayed in and went the distance. Leading off the bottom of the second inning against the Astros' starter, Holliday timed an outside pitch and lined it over the fence in right to give Carpenter a 1–0 lead. A homer in the top of the fourth by Carlos Lee made it 1–1. Although Holliday singled with a man on in the bottom of the frame, the game remained tied until the seventh. Carpenter, possessor of a .097 lifetime batting average at that point, ripped a fastball from reliever Jeff Fulchino into the left field corner for a double, advanced on a wild pitch, and scored easily on a long sacrifice fly by Julio Lugo to regain the lead, 2–1. Holliday gave Carp some insurance with a home run into the shrubbery in left center in the eighth, his third bomb in three games. After a one-two-three top of the ninth, the Redbirds were 3–1 winners. And Matt Holliday's early numbers as a Cardinal included a .606 batting average with three home runs, eight runs scored, and 10 RBIs in nine games.

With a few more good years, Matt Holliday could be headed to Cooperstown. But he might have played in the NFL instead. In high school he was his region's Gatorade Player of the Year in baseball and football. He was a quarterback and threw 65 touchdown passes. Dallas Cowboy coach Jimmy Johnson told Matt's father his son "couldn't miss."

CARDS GRAB WILD-CARD BERTH ON FINAL DAY

September 28, 2011

With five weeks remaining in the 2011 season, St. Louis's chances of making the playoffs were worse than remote. After losing three in a row to the Dodgers, the Cardinals were 10 games behind the division-leading Brewers and 10½ behind the wild-card leading Braves with 32 games to play. Although they then swept Milwaukee and Atlanta, the Redbirds were still 4½ games out of a playoff spot with 13 games left to play.

Though they closed ground by winning each of their final four series down the stretch, each loss seemed to dash any hope of catching the Braves. Two dramatic come-from-behind wins over the Mets were followed by a disastrous series finale in which the bullpen coughed up six runs in the ninth and lost the game 8–6. The next day, a three-run homer in the eighth inning by Alfonso Soriano snapped a 1–1 tie in the eighth inning, and the Cards fell to the Cubs. The loss left them three games behind with five to play. Chicago had a 1–0 ninth-inning lead in the next game before the Cubbies handed the Cards a 2–1 win with three walks, an error, and a walk-off wild pitch. St. Louis trailed in the series finale, as well, before Yadier Molina tied the score with a seventh-inning homer. Rafael Furcal's round-tripper in the eighth won the game, 3–2. The Braves, in the meantime, had lost a pair in Washington, so their lead was sliced to one game with three to play.

Atlanta hosted the powerful Philadelphia Phillies, NL East champions for the fifth season in a row. St. Louis finished up visiting the lowly Astros, who had already lost 104 games. In the first game at Minute Maid Park, former Astro Lance Berkman's two-run double in the eighth inning tied the game for the Cards, but an error by reliever Octavio Dotel preceded a walk-off squeeze bunt that gave Houston the 5–4 victory in 10 innings. Luckily, the Phils beat the Braves 4–2.

The 'Stros jumped on Jake Westbrook the next night for an early 5–0 lead, but the Birds roared back and won going away, 13–6. Atlanta took it on the chin 7–1, and the Cardinals and Braves entered the final

Courtesy Getty Images

scheduled date, Wednesday, September 28, tied for the wild-card lead. The Cardinals won their game easily, starting out with five consecutive hits against Brett Myers in a five-run first inning. Cardinals ace Chris Carpenter took it from there, pitching a two-hit, 8–0 shutout. Then the Cardinal players and Cardinals Nation watched nervously until the Phillies won out in Atlanta, 4–3 in 13 innings. Champagne soon splattered the visiting clubhouse in Houston, while living rooms and bars around St. Louis erupted in celebration. The Cardinals were in the playoffs!

Courtesy Getty Images

The Cards rallied in September (17–8), while Atlanta collapsed (9–17). On September 5, a website, coolstandings.com, gave the Cardinals a 1.5 percent chance of making the playoffs.

Considering the situation, it was the greatest game Carpenter ever pitched. He had made 350 starts and this was his only 1–0 shutout win. Tony La Russa said, "I think Carp will remember this forever . . . so will Cardinal fans."

1–0 CARPENTER GEM SENDS CARDINALS PAST PHILLIES

October 7, 2011

When St. Louis squeezed into the 2011 playoffs, its reward was a first-round matchup versus the Philadelphia Phillies, the team with the best regular-season record in baseball, 102–60. Coming from behind to win games 2 and 4, the Cardinals forced a decisive contest in the best-of-five series. It was a classic matchup of aces, Chris Carpenter for the Cardinals and Roy "Doc" Halladay for the Phillies. Doc had given up a three-run homer in the first inning of Game 1 but had finished strong, retiring the last 21 Cardinals batters he had faced. Carp, starting in Game 2, had been raked for four runs in three innings pitched. The two were still close friends from their days in the Toronto organization together, and this would be the first time they had pitched against one another.

The Cardinals got an early boost when leadoff man Rafael Furcal hit a drive over center fielder Shane Victorino's head. The ball short-hopped the wall near the 398 sign, and Furcal raced around second base. The Phils lost a chance to get him at third when Victorino's relay skipped under second baseman Chase Utley's glove. Furcal got a triple with a head-first slide. Skip Schumaker, a surprise starter in center field in Tony La Russa's lineup, fell behind in the count but proceeded to foul off five two-strike pitches from Halladay. Finally, he got a pitch up and in and lined it into the right field corner for a run-scoring double. It took Halladay 32 pitches to get through the first inning, but he breezed through the next six rounds, scattering three hits and walking none. The Cards loaded the bases in the eighth, but Lance Berkman and Matt Holliday could not get a run in.

It would be up to Carpenter to hold a 1–0 lead against a lineup of nine players, all of whom were All-Stars at one time or another. After three quick innings, a leadoff hit batsman and a two-out single put Phillies on the corners in the fourth. Raúl Ibañez, a savvy hitter, worked the count full before slamming an outside pitch deep to right. Luckily for Carp, the ball was just a little too high and was caught on the warning track. Philadelphia got only two runners after that, and one of those was cut down stealing by catcher Yadier Molina. Shortstop Furcal robbed Phillie catcher Carlos Ruiz with a sensational diving stop up the middle in the eighth.

When Ryan Howard grounded out to end the game, Carpenter let out a triumphant roar and led his teammates in a group bounce near first base. The Cardinals had beaten the mighty Phillies. Now they felt they could beat anybody.

Courtesy Don Korte

FREESE'S HEROICS GIVE CARDINALS EPIC VICTORY IN GAME 6

October 27, 2011

It was one of the most dramatic games in World Series history and one of the most dramatic in the long annals of Cardinals' lore. Facing elimination in Game 6 of the 2011 World Series, the St. Louis Cardinals fell behind the Texas Rangers but rallied to tie the score on five different occasions. Twice the Redbirds were down to their last strike, and twice they came through. Finally, an 11th-inning home run by David Freese won the game for St. Louis.

The game had seesawed from the start. Texas scored once in the top of the first, and St. Louis answered with a two-run homer by Lance Berkman in the bottom. Single runs in the second and fourth put the Rangers ahead again, but a Redbird rally in the fourth made it 3–3.

An error by Freese on an easy pop-up helped the Rangers go back ahead by a run in the fifth inning. St. Louis tied the score at 4–4 in the sixth on a bases-loaded walk. In the seventh, Texas went ahead 7–4 with three runs off Lance Lynn, pitching in relief of Jaime Garcia. The first two came on back-to-back home runs by Adrian Beltre and Nelson Cruz. Allen Craig hit a solo homer in the eighth to cut the deficit to 7–5, but the Cardinals left the bases loaded.

Ranger closer Neftali Feliz came in to protect the two-run lead in the ninth and struck out the first hitter. Albert Pujols then doubled to left center, and Berkman walked on four pitches, putting the tying runs on base. When Craig was called out on strikes, Freese came up as the Cardinals' last hope. He fell behind in the count, 1–2, before lifting a drive deep to right field. Texas outfielder Cruz drifted back toward the wall but could not make the catch. The ball bounced off the wall, and Freese had a two-run, game-tying triple.

The Rangers went right back into the lead in the top of the 10th, on a two-run home run by Josh Hamilton. Two Cardinals hits and two infield outs plated one runner but brought the Rangers to within one out of the title again. With men on first and second and two out and the count two and two,

Berkman came through with a liner over the second baseman to tie the game again.

After Jake Westbrook blanked the Rangers in the top of the 11th, Freese led off the bottom half against Mark Lowe, the eighth Texas hurler of the night. A full-count pitch was down in the batter's wheelhouse, and Freese blasted it to straightaway center field for a walk-off home run. The Busch Stadium crowd went from frazzled to delirious. Having overcome five different deficits, and after being down to their final strike in two different innings, the Cardinals had somehow survived and won the game, 10–9.

Courtesy Herkievia via Flickr

Freese's game will live in Cardinals lore forever. However, if Lance Berkman, also down to the team's last strike, hadn't driven in the tying run in the 10th, Freese would not have had the chance for the historic walk-off homer. ESPN baseball analyst Buster Olney called it the greatest game in baseball history.

Courtesy Don Korte

11 IN '11: CARDINALS WIN SERIES IN SEVEN

October 28, 2011

Riding the momentum of their heart-pounding victory in Game 6, the St. Louis Cardinals beat the Texas Rangers in Game 7 of the 2011 World Series to capture the franchise's 11th world championship. The final score of the final game was 6–2, and the heroes were starting and winning pitcher Chris Carpenter plus hitting stars who added to their Game 6 exploits: David Freese, Allen Craig, and Yadier Molina.

Although the Rangers had suffered a wrenching defeat on Thursday, they came out firing in the decisive game on Friday. Ian Kinsler opened against Carpenter with a line-drive single. But he was picked off by the well-practiced duo of Molina to Pujols. Undaunted, the Rangers kept up the attack with a walk and RBI doubles by Josh Hamilton and Michael Young before Carpenter could close out the inning.

Texas starter Matt Harrison retired the first two Cardinals hitters in the bottom of the first but then walked Albert Pujols and Lance Berkman. With three balls and two strikes, David Freese further enhanced his mushrooming legend by splitting the gap in left center for a game-tying, two-run double.

Texas led the series three games to two, and the champagne was iced in the Rangers' locker room. Texas family members gleefully walked past the KMOX radio studio under the stadium to a room and prepared to celebrate. Then, David Freese took over. The Rangers were so devastated from losing Game 6 that they had little chance in Game 7.

Courtesy Getty Images

In the top of the second, a single and a two-out walk had Carpenter in trouble again, and pitching coach Dave Duncan came to the mound for a brief talk. Carp got out of the inning and began to use his breaking ball to better effect as the game went on.

On the other hand, Harrison was burned by another full-count pitch in the third inning, which Craig lofted into the right field bullpen for a home run. It would turn out to be Craig's third game-winning RBI of the series. In the fifth inning, the Texas bullpen handed the Cardinals two runs on no hits. Scott Feldman hit one man with a pitch and walked three other hitters, forcing home a run. And C. J. Wilson's first pitch hit Rafael Furcal, forcing in another run. St. Louis now led 5–2. Molina added an RBI single in the seventh.

Carpenter had a one–two–three top of the sixth, but two balls were hit hard, including a potential home run by Nelson Cruz that left fielder Craig turned into an out with a leaping catch with his back against the wall. After giving up a leadoff double in the seventh, Carpenter was removed. Bullpen men Arthur Rhodes, Octavio Dotel, Lance Lynn, and Jason Motte combined for nine straight outs to close out the game.

Courtesy Don Korte

Having been all but dead in the wild-card race, the Cardinals had trailed in all three postseason series before winning each round. It was an unexpected and delightful ending for Tony La Russa's managerial career—world championship number eleven in '11.

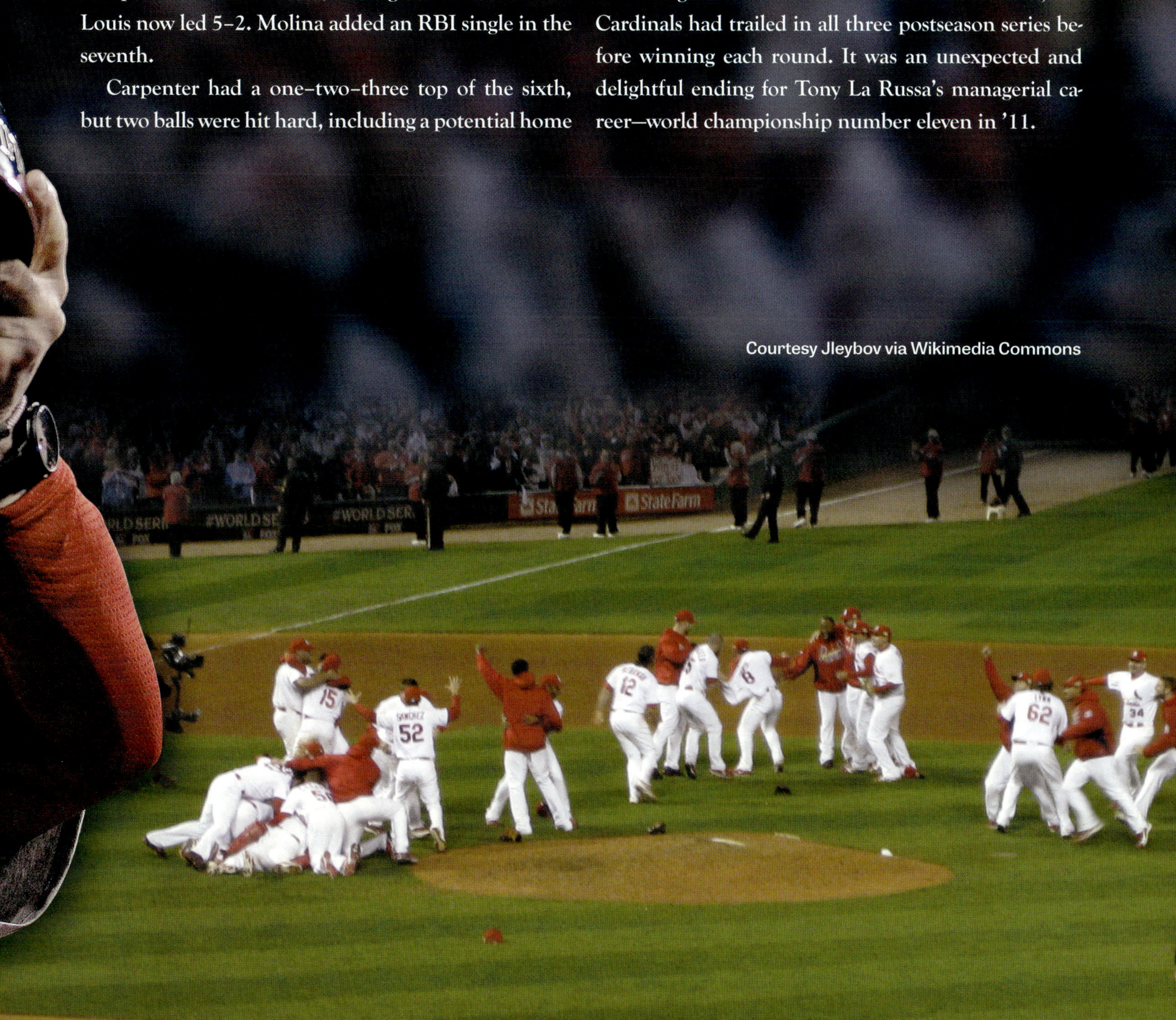

Courtesy Jleybov via Wikimedia Commons

ANOTHER CARDINALS MIRACLE SINKS NATIONALS

October 12, 2012

The new Cardinals paradigm: another elimination game, another miracle comeback. Down 6–0 after three innings and still down 7–5 through eight, the Cards rallied to beat the Washington Nationals to win the decisive Game 5 of the National League Division Series, 9–7, and move on to the NLCS.

Tied two games apiece in the best-of-five series, the Nats had their pitching ace starting the deciding game, lefty Gio Gonzalez, a 21-game winner in the regular season. He would be opposed by Adam Wainwright, 14–13 on the season after missing a year due to elbow surgery. Wainwright did not have it on this day. In the bottom of the first, the Nationals led off with a double, triple, and home run, in order, to build a 3–0 lead after just seven pitches. In the Washington third inning, Bryce Harper and Michael Morse hit long home runs, making it 6–0, and Wainwright's day was over.

Trailing 6–0, it looked as if the Cardinals season was over as well. But Matt Holliday's RBI double to left got the Cardinals their first run in the fourth. Daniel Descalso and Pete Kozma got hits to start the Redbird fifth, and they eventually scored on a wild pitch and a bases-loaded walk, cutting the deficit to 6–3. In the seventh, Carlos Beltran doubled home Jon Jay to make it 6–4. And Descalso's homer in the eighth brought St. Louis to within one run.

Cardinals relievers Joe Kelly, Trevor Rosenthal, Edward Mujica, and Mitchell Boggs had held the Nationals to no runs and just one hit from the third through the seventh. Closer Jason Motte, however, gave up a run in the bottom of the eighth on three singles.

So Washington led 7–5 when closer Drew Storen took over their pitching duties in the top of the ninth. Beltran greeted him with a double to center, capping a three-for-three day with two walks for the veteran switch-hitter. Two quick outs brought the Nats to within one out of victory. They got within one strike on each of the next two batters, but both Yadier Molina and David Freese walked on 3–2 pitches. Suddenly the go-ahead runs were on base for Descalso, who sent a hard grounder up the middle. Shortstop Ian Desmond lunged for the ball and deflected it into no-man's land in center field. As the tying runs scored, the Washington crowd went silent. Descalso stole second base, and one pitch later Kozma lined a hit down the right field line to drive home two go-ahead runs. A few Cardinals fans could be heard cheering in the otherwise funereal ballpark.

Courtesy Keith Allison via Wikipedia Commons

Motte came out again in the bottom of the ninth and went through the top of the Nationals' order, one-two-three, to close out another improbable, last-strike Cardinals victory.

> ***Historic playoff comebacks seem to be in the Cardinals DNA. They scored four runs in the ninth inning to beat the Nationals. Here's a trivia question that could win some bets. Who were the players who drove in the four runs? (Daniel Descalso and Pete Kozma)***

ADAMS STEPS UP WITH TWO HOMERS IN EXTRA INNINGS

September 4, 2013

In seven disastrous days late in the summer of 2013, the Cardinals lost five out of six games against the Pirates and Reds, their National League Central rivals, falling behind Pittsburgh and coming dangerously close to dropping behind Cincinnati as well. Worse still, St. Louis's RBI leader Allen Craig injured his ankle late in the Cincy series and missed the rest of the regular season. But in the same game in which Craig went down, young Matt Adams stepped up and hit two big home runs in extra innings to win a 16-inning marathon versus the Reds.

It happened on September 4 at Great American Ball Park. The Reds scored two runs in the second inning. In the Cardinals fourth, singles by Matt Carpenter and Carlos Beltran put men at the corners. On Matt Holliday's sacrifice fly, Carpenter scored and Beltran alertly moved up to second base. This allowed him to score on the next play, an infield hit by Allen Craig compounded by a throwing error by Cincinnati first baseman Joey Votto. Seeing the wild throw, Craig tried to change course for second base, but as he hit the bag at first, he turned his right ankle inwards. He was tagged out as he lay on the ground in pain. Brandon Phillips put the home team ahead with a home run in the fifth. But in the top of the sixth, Carpenter added to his league-leading figures in hits, doubles, and runs scored, and Beltran provided the RBI.

Slippery Rock University is not exactly a baseball factory. Adams is one of two from that university to play in the majors. Coincidentally, the other one, Doc Marshall, played parts of three seasons (1907, '08, '09) with the Cardinals. A catcher, he had two big league home runs.

Starters Bronson Arroyo for Cincinnati and Shelby Miller for St. Louis were gone by the eighth inning, and the bullpens rang up matching zeroes far into the night. In the top of the 14th, Reds right-hander Alfredo Simon faced the Cardinals cleanup spot leading off. Substituting for the injured Craig was Matt Adams, who was in an zero-for-17 dry spell. In this at-bat, however, Simon let a fastball drift over the middle of the plate, and the left-handed-hitting Adams lined it into the bleachers in a blink, a 394-foot home run. Alas, Cardinals closer Edward Mujica could not convert the save. Minor league base-stealing phenom Billy Hamilton swiped second as a pinch runner and scored on a single to reknot the count at 4–4.

In the 16th inning, Adams did it again, dropping the bat head on a low inside fastball from Logan Ondrusek for a 403-foot thunderbolt home run. This time Carlos Martinez was able to finish up with a scoreless bottom of the inning. Not only had the Cardinals won a long, tough game, they had found out that the loss of Craig might not be fatal to their pennant hopes. Indeed, with Adams as first baseman, the Cardinals finished 17–6 in the final weeks to win the Central.

Courtesy Getty Images

WACHA AND CARDS TROUNCE DODGERS TO WIN NL PENNANT

October 18, 2013

When the Cardinals beat the Dodgers in the 2013 National League Championship Series, the baseball nova called Michael Wacha glowed even brighter. The rookie shut out Los Angeles for the first seven innings of the clinching Game 6, and with two rookie relief pitchers finishing up, St. Louis won easily at home, 9–0. It was the second time in the series that Wacha had beaten Dodger Cy Young Award–winner Clayton Kershaw.

Besides beating LA 1–0 in Game 2 of the NLCS, Wacha had staved off elimination in the first round playoff series against the Pirates. The rookie got the 2–1 win after taking a no-hitter into the eighth inning. Prior to that, in his final regular-season start, Wacha had come within one out of a no-hitter versus the Nationals.

Although the Cardinals led the best-of-seven NLCS three games to two, St. Louis had uneasy memories from the previous October, when the Redbirds had blown a three-games-to-one lead and lost the NL championship to the Giants. If the Cardinals lost Game 6, Dodger lefty Hyun-Jin Ryu loomed for Game 7, the same Ryu who had baffled the St. Louis lineup in a 3–0 loss in Game 3.

After Dodger leadoff hitter Carl Crawford got an infield hit to start the game, Wacha buzzed through the rest of the LA lineup. In the first two innings, Kershaw gave up two hits and bounced two wild pitches but kept St. Louis scoreless. With one out in the bottom of the third, Matt Carpenter, the Cards' slumping leadoff man, went to battle against Kershaw. He fouled off five two-strike pitches before smacking the 11th pitch of the at-bat to the gap in right center for a double. Carlos Beltran drove Carpenter home with a single past the second baseman, and when right fielder Yasiel Puig's throw toward home was muffed, Beltran cruised to second. After a strikeout, the Cardinals dissected Kershaw's deliveries for three more hits and two walks. With another bad throw by Puig in the mix, the Cardinals came out of the inning with a 4–0 lead. In the top of the fifth, old man Beltran laid out in right center to rob Juan Uribe of extra bases.

St. Louis put the game away with five runs in the fifth inning. Solid hits by the first three batters—Yadier Molina, David Freese, and Matt Adams—pushed one run across and knocked Kershaw out of the game. As the Los Angeles defense continued to foozle, the Cardinals plated four more runs on just one more hit.

Wacha pitched seven innings, allowing no runs, two hits, and one walk. Carlos Martinez in the eighth and Trevor Rosenthal in the ninth completed the 9–0 shutout, sending St. Louis to the World Series for the fourth time in the last 10 seasons.

Wacha began the 2013 season in the minors, but in a magical year he won the NLCS MVP award to begin his major league career. Through the NLCS, he allowed just one run on eight hits in 21 innings for a 0.43 ERA while striking out 22.

Courtesy Johnmaxmena2 via Wikimedia Commons

CARPENTER BOMBARDS WRIGLEY WITH THREE HOMERS AND TWO DOUBLES

July 20, 2018

Matt Carpenter's 2018 season got off to a miserable start. He started the season batting third in the lineup, and nothing went right. His batting average bottomed out at .140 in mid-May. But when he was restored a more comfortable spot as leadoff man, his season turned around. Using his scythe-wielder uppercut swing, his average and power both grew, and more than half his hits went for extra bases. By the All-Star break he had crept into the National League's top ten in doubles and home runs.

His surge reached its crescendo in the second game after the break in Chicago. On a Friday afternoon, the Cardinals won a laugher, 18–5, and Carp became just the second player in big league history to hit three homers and two doubles in the same game.

Carpenter faced Cub lefthander Jon Lester to open the game. With a couple of fouls, Carp worked the count full before blasting a fastball off of the right field video board in Wrigley for a no-doubt home run. In the second frame, the Red Birds had scored two runs before Carpenter came up with one on and two out. This time he golfed a two-strike fastball into the middle of the bleachers in right, upping the St. Louis lead to 5–0.

St. Louis scored seven more runs in the fourth inning to open up a 12–1 lead. Carpenter's contribution was two doubles, one to left center to start the rally and other to right center to cap the scoring.

With the big lead, interim manager Mike Shildt, in only his third game as skipper, suggested that Carpenter take the rest of the day off. Matt was agreeable, but when his spot in the batting order came up with two outs and two on in the top of the sixth, he decided to take one more at bat. Though his first four hits had all come with two strikes, Matt jumped on lefty Brian Duensing's first pitch and lofted a high fly toward the right field corner. The drive just barely reached the Wrigley bleacher basket, giving him his third home run and fifth extra base hit of the day. Carpenter then left the game.

With a doubleheader looming on Saturday, the Cubs saved their relief pitchers by using three different position players on the mound in the last three innings. If Carpenter had stayed in the game, he most likely would have faced a "pitcher" whose "fastballs" topped out in the high 60s m.p.h.

Matt's hot hitting continued for six more weeks. He won NL Player of the Month honors in July. By mid-August he was leading the league in home runs and was a leading MVP candidate. Unfortunately, Carpenter's batting magic disappeared; his September numbers showed a .170 average with just one homer.

The Cardinals were the last National League team eliminated from playoff contention.

Cardinal fans cheered through Matt Carpenter's seven productive years as a leadoff man. They also remember his almost catastrophic collapse at the plate that followed. His 2018 average of .257 (with 36 homers) nosedived over the next three years to .226, .186, and .169. "Nobody is more disappointed than me," he confessed. Injuries in 2022 with the Yankees and in 2024 with the Cardinals added more frustration to his career.

Courtesy Getty Images

Courtesy Getty Images

YADI SAVES THE SEASON: KEY AT-BATS BRING VICTORY IN AN ELIMINATION GAME

October 7, 2019

Trailing the Braves in the best-of-five first round playoff series two games to one, the Cardinals survived with a white-knuckle victory, 5–4 in 10 innings. Manager Mike Shildt used eight pitchers, Marcel Ozuna hit a pair of homers, and Paul Goldschmidt had a four-bagger and two doubles. But in the end, the biggest hero for St. Louis was the revered veteran catcher Yadier Molina. Yadi stroked a game-tying hit with two out in the eighth inning and drove home the game-winning run with a sacrifice fly in the 10th, sending the Busch Stadium crowd into flights of ecstasy.

The Red Birds had won the series opener but lost the next two games while scoring just one run. In Game 4 they got a pair of tallies in the bottom of the first one back-to-back home runs by Goldschmidt and Ozuna. Atlanta got one run against St. Louis starter Dakota Hudson in the third inning. But another Ozuna homer in the fourth gave the Cards a brief 3–1 lead.

In the top of the fifth, Atlanta jumped ahead 4–3 thanks to a fluke double, a passed ball by Molina, an error by third baseman Matt Carpenter, and a two-run home run by Ozzie Albies. Tyler Webb relieved Hudson and fanned Braves slugger Freddie Freeman to end the round. Atlanta loaded the bases in each of the next two frames, but Red Bird relievers John Brebbia and Andrew Miller kept them from scoring. Ryan Helsley struck out three Braves in a row in the eighth.

Time was running out on the season when Goldschmidt came to bat with one out in the bottom of the eighth. Jammed on the fists by a pitch, Goldy had just enough bat speed to float a hit over the third baseman and just enough foot speed to leg out a broken-bat double. Ozuna fanned for the second out, leaving it up to Molina to drive in the run. Eying the open spaces in right field, Yadi flicked his bat at the first pitch. First baseman Freeman made a valiant leap, but the soft liner just tipped off his glove and fell in safely, allowing Goldschmidt to ramble home with the tying run.

Carlos Martinez, who had been hit hard in this series, yielded a leadoff double in the ninth but buckled down and retired the next three hitters in a row. Miles Mikolas pitched a one-two-three top of the 10th. In the bottom, Kolten Wong led off with a double and moved to third with one out. The crowd was on its feet as Molina stepped to the plate. Again, Yadi came through on the first pitch, lofting a long fly to left field that scored Wong easily with the game-winning run. Molina flung his bat into the outfield and was mobbed by his doting teammates, while the crowd serenaded him from the stands.

"YADI, YADI, YADI!"

It would be inaccurate to call Yadier Molina a great hitter. But Yadi was considered a tough out with the ability to get the big RBI. Even with glacier-like running speed, he hammered out 2,168 career hits and a .277 batting average. His 19-year career with St. Louis glittered with Gold and Platinum gloves, making him an icon for Cardinal Nation.

Courtesy Getty Images

MASKED MEN HUGGING

August 30, 2020

The COVID-19 restrictions in 2020 hurt the Cardinals more than any other big league team. All teams were shut down from before St. Patrick's Day until mid summer. The 60-game "regular season" began in late July. But five games into that schedule, positive COVID-19 tests put the Cardinal team into quarantine. The squad spent over two weeks isolated, no meetings and no workouts, until the middle of August. When they finally resumed play, they had only 44 days in which to play 54 games.

In the next two weeks, they played four doubleheaders, and their bullpen was nearing exhaustion. By August 30 they were riding a four-game losing streak and had slipped below .500 in the standings. At this critical juncture, Adam Wainwright stepped into the breach. The veteran was the oldest active player in the National League, and August 30th happened to be his 39th birthday. Early that day, he told members of the bullpen that he would give the relievers the day off. These were brave words to be sure, since Wainwright had not pitched a complete game since 2016. After an injury-filled season in 2018, many thought his pitching days were over. But he had bounced back nicely in 2019.

His birthday start in 2020 coincided with a pair of milestones for his long-time mate Yadier Molina, who was playing in his 2000th regular-season game as a Cardinal and got two hits to pass Red Schoendienst for sixth place on the Cards' career hit list.

Wainwright struggled in the early going, needing 57 pitches to complete three innings. He yielded a two-run home run to Cleveland's Tyler Naquin to fall behind in the second inning. But a pair of two-run hits by Dexter Fowler and Dylan Carlson gave St. Louis a 4–2 lead in the bottom of the round. The Cardinals added a run in the third on a double by Paul Goldschmidt and a run-scoring balk.

Wainwright finally settled down, however, and he faced only one man over the minimum in the last six innings. Meanwhile, his teammates added single runs in the seventh and eighth innings. The tall right-hander had his famous Uncle Charlie curveball slicing through the strike zone all afternoon. Of his nine Ks in the game, six came on called third strikes.

Before going out for the 9th inning, Waino and Yadi both stuck surgical masks in their pockets. After a quick one–two–three final frame, both men masked up and shared a long heartfelt embrace on the mound. Since the only "fans" in the stands were paper cutouts, the only cheering came from the dugouts, as both the Cardinal and Indian players saluted the Old Man. Wainwright wiped back tears in his postgame interview as he extolled "my brother" (Molina) and reflected on the doubts and struggles he had gone through to once again become the Cardinals pitching ace.

Baseball is a game welded together by numbers — statistics. Adam Wainwright and Yadier Molina's record of 328 starts together seems unbreakable. Never say never? SAY NEVER! Molina caught in 2,138 Wainwright's innings and 1,812 of his strikeouts. On top of that, they are best friends.

17-GAME STREAK LIFTS CARDS TO POSTSEASON

September 18, 2021

The Cardinals spent most of the summer of 2021 hovering around the .500 mark, trailing in both the division and wild card standings. But in September a team-record 17 consecutive wins boosted St. Louis into the postseason as a wild card team. There were heroes up and down the roster during the historic streak.

After losing a series opener at home to Cincinnati on September 10, St. Louis had a record of 71–69, three and a half games out of the last wild card spot. On Saturday the 11, they spotted the Reds a four-run lead but came back to win 6–4. The next day they won 2–0. Nolan Arenado was the hero with go-ahead two-run homers in each victory. Then it was off to New York, where the Cardinals won three in a row from the fading Mets. The Red Bird defense was sensational, turning six double plays and getting highlight-reel performances from Lars Nootbaar in right field and Paul Goldschmidt at first base. And the St. Louis bats slammed out 41 hits. With the sweep, the Cardinals passed the Reds and Padres to take the lead for the last playoff spot.

Back home against San Diego, another three-game sweep pushed the Padres farther back. Left fielder Tyler O'Neill bashed a pair of clutch two-run homers, while right fielder Dylan Carlson chipped in with a pair on dingers of his own (including a grand slam) and a critical throw that thwarted a Padre rally. When the Cardinals arrived in Milwaukee for four games, the Brewers needed only two more wins to clinch the Central Division title. But the Brew Crew was overwhelmed by the Red Bird squad. Arenado reached 100 RBIs on the season, John Lester got his 200th career win, and Adam Wainwright reached 2,000 career strikeouts. In a 2–1 win, Nootbaar and Tommy Edman each scored after stealing second base. And in the series finale Goldschmidt's two home runs keyed a rally from a 5–0 deficit.

Four more wins in Chicago followed, growing the streak to 16 in a row, breaking the old St. Louis National League record of 14 straight. Center fielder Harrison Bader led the charge at Wrigley with a 10-for-15 series, including three homers, eight runs scored, and another eight batted in. The highlight of the sweep was an incredible three–two–five–four–two–eight–six double play started by Goldy that preserved a one-run lead.

When the final homestand of the season opened on September 28, the Cardinals needed only one more win to clinch a playoff berth. They got it that night with a 6–2 verdict versus Milwaukee. Wainwright gave up an early two-run homer but went six innings to get his 17th win of the season. He also contributed a neat squeeze bunt to aid the Cardinal comeback. Carlson, Arenado, and Jose Rondon all homered. Giovanny Gallegos closed out the game for the ninth time during the streak, and the Cards celebrated their historic 17th consecutive win with champagne.

The New York Giants won 26 in a row, with a tie in the middle (the tie game was replayed from the start the next day, with New York winning). In the last 100 years, the Cleveland Indians won 22 straight in 2017, the Cubs ran off 21 in a row in 1935, and Oakland captured 20 straight in 2002.

Courtesy Getty Images

ALBERT'S FANTASTIC FINISH

October 2, 2022

Just nine days before the start of the 2022 season, Albert Pujols signed to play with the St. Louis Cardinals. From the start Albert made it clear this would be his final season as a player. Cardinal Nation was euphoric about seeing number 5 with the Birds on the Bat after 10 years away.

At 42, Pujols was the oldest player in the majors and his numbers had climbed to the very top rungs of career achievement. Already fifth all time with 679 home runs, he needed 17 more catch Alex Rodriguez at number four. But the big target was 700 homers. Before the season was out, he would not only pass the home run milestones, he would climb to second place all time in both total bases and RBIs, passing a couple of guys named Musial and Ruth. At the finish, he was the hottest hitter in baseball. Eight of his final nine homers either tied the score or put the Cardinals ahead. And in his last 10 plate appearances he had nine RBIs!

Smiling all season long, he relished the role of Uncle Albert, happy to counsel younger players. But at the end of June he had only four home runs and a .198 batting average, and reaching 700 seemed unattainable. Still, he was chosen as a legacy pick for the All Star Game. The honor seemed to stir his old bones, and Pujols hit two homers in the next week.

At the All-Star festivities at Dodger Stadium, the younger players doted on him, and Pujols stole the show. When he won the first round of the Home Run Derby against eventual NL home run champ Kyle Schwarber, the loser gladly bowed in respect. Always a workaholic, Albert had adjusted his swing by cutting down on his hand movement and altering the bat angle in his stance. It paid big dividends in the second half of the season. In August, he pumped out seven dingers, six against lefties. One of them moved him past Stan the Man for number two in career total bases, trailing only Henry Aaron. His 700th home run now seemed within reach.

Numbers 699 and 700 came in Los Angeles on Friday, September 23, with a crowd of 50,000 cheering him. The milestone blast came with two on and one out in the fouth inning on a hanging slider from Phil Bickford. His last homer in St. Louis was a drive into the grassy center field backdrop at Busch on October 2. It came in the emotion-packed final home game of the regular season. Shortly after his blast, Pujols was removed from the game alongside his old mates and friends Yadier Molina and Adam Wainwright.

Still, Albert was not done. He added one more home run, his 703rd, in Pittsburgh, and that two-run bomb moved him past the immortal Babe Ruth into second place on the all-time runs batted in list. What a way to go out!

Few major leaguers played 22 years as consistently as Albert Pujols, and his final flourish allowed him to tie another baseball legend. In his rookie season in 2001, he hit 31 home runs. In his last season, he hit 24 homers. Only one other player in history who played more than 10 seasons hit 20 or more home runs in both his first and last seasons. That player was Ted Williams.

Courtesy Getty Images

INDEX